MASONICA

A Guide for Craft a... ..... Speech Making

Banqueting goes back to time immemorial
16th-century print of William I

MASONICALLY SPEAKING

A Guide for Craft and other Speech Making

Yasha Beresiner

www.thefreemason.com
+44 (0) 870 922 0352

*This book is dedicated with total love and affection
to Abigail and Noah who brought constant sunshine
and smiles when they came into this world.*

Extra Special For Masons Only
Cuba Cigar Box Label 1900 (YB)

FRONT COVER
Cagliostro caught out
Gilray 18th century
(Library and Museum of Freemasonry)

First published 2007

ISBN (10) 0 8531 8 274 4

ISBN (13) 978 0 8531 8 274 0

© Yasha Beresiner 2007

Published by Lewis Masonic

an imprint of Ian Allan Publishing Ltd, Hersham, Surrey KT12 4RG.

Printed in England by Ian Allan Printing Ltd, Hersham, Surrey KT12 4RG

Code: 0708/

Visit the Lewis Masonic website at www.lewismasonic.com

The Menu
Contents

Pre-Dinner Drinks
Anon 18th-century print (Guildhall)

Introduction

When you browse through the history of our remarkable craft, you will find it impossible to get away from eating, drinking, food and speeches from the very start. After all, *organised* Freemasonry began in June 1717 around a dining table at the Goose and Gridiron in London, and seven decades earlier, in the early evening of the 16 October 1646, Elias Ashmole wined and dined, following his initiation in Warrington. He stood, took a deep breath and, somewhat nervously notwithstanding his legal training, conveyed his thanks to those assembled at dinner in his father-in-law's home in Warrington. It was the first Masonic speech and we all follow in his footsteps. From the very start, the Premier Grand Lodge wasted no time to decide on two Grand Masters a year, elected every six months so that the brethren could enjoy two major festivals annually. Little has changed over the centuries. We may have moved from ceremonies conducted around the dining table at inns and taverns to purpose-built lodge rooms and sophisticated dining halls, but a most important aspect of English Freemasonry remains the festive board and its after proceedings.

That is what this book is all about. The content applies equally, with logical adaptation, to Craft, Royal Arch and Mark as well as other Orders and organisations. Historical facts will give you 'fillers' for your speech, as will the anecdotes. Please do not look for new never-before-told stories: there is no such thing as a new story. It is only a question as to whether you have or have not heard it before. The tales I tell are tried, tested and successful and a good story is always worth repeating. For the best part of a half-century, I have collected stories and anecdotes from umpteen sources and more recently from the Internet. I acknowledge my gratitude to all the providers not mentioned in the bibliography and credits. I would not want any originality to be interpreted as undetected plagiarism. I have added an extended chapter on *Talks and Lectures* – this will complete the guidelines and instructions that I am able to convey on the subject of speaking. The summarised listing at the end of each chapter is intended for reference and practical use.

⟁ **1**
Throughout my career I had many opportunities for spontaneous off-the-cuff speeches, which were a great success because they were always well rehearsed.

Ceremonies are many fold and varied
King caricature 1830 (Guildhall)

Understanding the true significance of this paradox has served me well: there is no perfect natural speaker, no more than there is anyone who *cannot* become an excellent speaker. All it needs is a little hard work and lots of practice. As you read along, I will be flooding you with advice and counsel and ask that you constantly bear in mind the two basic essentials to be a good speaker: a knowledge of your subject, and confidence.

2

A newly elected member of parliament was about to stand to deliver his maiden speech. He turned to his mentor sitting next to him and asked to borrow a £50 note for the few minutes he would be speaking. He placed the money in his shirt pocket and stood to deliver an inspiring and very well received first speech. As he sat down, he handed the £50 back to his companion explaining, "When you have money in your pocket, you speak a different language."

This is what confidence does and confidence comes with knowledge of your subject, be it a brief toast to a brother or an extended lecture on Masonic jurisprudence. An after-dinner speaker is a raconteur, a storyteller. Humour is, of course, an essential spice and I will be glad to assist with that aspect, too. Finally, I trust the reader will allow me some artistic licence with my history and content of anecdotes, as deep down I know I am quite superficial.

Enjoy your dinner, even if you are the speaker . . .

Pre-dinner Drinks:
Preparation

1717 and all that

Although there are no contemporary records of the start of organised Freemasonry, it is generally accepted that beyond charity, a festive board and related socialising was the *raison d'être* of the early membership of our fraternity. It was only with James Anderson's second *Constitutions of 1738*, twenty-one years after the formation of Grand Lodge, that a detailed report on the events that took place on that momentous and historic 24 June 1717 became available. Four London lodges met at a festive table in the Goose and Gridiron tavern to found the Premier Grand Lodge of England, the first Grand Lodge in the world. And we have not looked back since. Anderson was not present at the foundation, and since there were no news reports at the time, he had to rely on hearsay for detailed information. All the available hearsay indicated that our founding fathers placed an emphasis on dining. In England, to some extent, we continue in the same vein today.

Refreshment

There have always been lodges formed by the common interests of the brethren who founded them – research lodges and academic ones, musicians and school lodges, lawyers and accountants, police and the military, and many more.

3
One of the most impressive meetings I have had the privilege of addressing was a military lodge in the south of England where the majority of the brethren wore their full uniforms. I was somewhat disconcerted when, ten minutes into my lecture, I saw the Senior Warden remove his pistol from its holster and place it on the pedestal in front of him. I tried to ignore the action and continued speaking when, some minutes later, I noticed the Junior Warden do the same. I stopped talking and turned to the Master. "Is everything in order, Worshipful Master?" I enquired. "Oh yes," he replied. "You carry on speaking, Bro Beresiner. The guns are intended for the brother who invited you to speak here."

The majority of lodges have always had some refreshment after their meetings. Outside of London in the 18th and 19th centuries where the brethren would have had some distance to travel, meetings were held during the day or as near to the full moon as possible. Speeches would have had to be curtailed.

4
The brother responding on behalf of the visitors had exceeded his allotted time and had the appearance of planning to go on for some time yet. The Master signalled his Warden with the gavel, implying that a gentle tap to the speaker's head may encourage him to sit down. The Warden, obedient to his Master's command, crept behind the speaker, and as he was about to hit him, tripped and the gavel landed on the head of a brother sitting next to the speaker. Knocked semi-conscious, he slid under the table and was heard to say, "Hit me again! I can still hear him speak."

The repast in an ordinary Provincial Lodge would have been informal in the 1800s. Extant records give the menu: cottage loaves, cheese, pickled onions and large quantities of beer in a warm and friendly ambiance. London, the metropolis that it was by Victorian times, had a greater concentration of lodges and Masons and held far more elaborate dinners. The fact that the Victorian middle classes were big eaters is reflected in the surviving menus, especially of Installation and Consecration meetings. It would not be unusual to have a menu with ten courses, giving alternative choices for many of the dishes and a selection of wines and liqueurs to assist with digestion.

Entertainment

Music was very much part of the Masonic dinner scene of the period. Anderson, in his first *Constitutions*, encouraged it by publishing words and music for the benefit of the brethren. Available records of the mid-1700s show members of the lodge singing to the accompaniment of a violin or flute. Towards the end of the century and start of the nineteenth in London and other large cities such as Manchester and Birmingham, well-known professional performers, string quartets, solo violinists, cellists and male and female vocalists, were hired to entertain the brethren. They all offered their services in contemporary advertisements published in the Masonic press. Entertainment extended to areas beyond the dining table. Many Masonic golf, cricket, bowling and similar sport associations met and competed in a refreshingly non-Masonic environment.

Speeches

You may be surprised to find that we are blessed by brevity today, compared to the 19th century. Twelve toasts was the norm at an installation banquet and eight of them were replied to. "Has he finished his speech?" was the question. "He finished his speech long ago," came the reply. "But he hasn't stopped talking." You cannot be too well prepared as a speaker. The more information you gather and the more observation you apply, the more confidence you will gain. Confidence, I repeat, is an essential element for a good speech. We will consider the content and shape of your speech in chapter V. Here concentrate on your physical and practical preparations. You are, hopefully, embarking on a long speaking career. Once you have mastered the art, it will serve you for the whole of your life and may it be long. My family have a tradition of longevity.

5
We have written evidence of my grandfather Joseph applying for life insurance on his 90th birthday, which, to his dismay, he was refused because of his age. "How can that be?" he persisted with the clerk. "Only yesterday my father was here and you gave him life cover." "Your father!" exclaimed the naturally surprised insurance clerk. "How old is your father?" he asked. "I don't know exactly," replied granddad Joseph. "He is well over 100." The clerk consented to take details. "Please come back on Wednesday and we will sort all this out for you," he said. "Wednesday is out of the question," granddad retorted. "My grandparents are getting married and I have to be at the wedding." The clerk was naturally incredulous. "Your grandparents are getting married?" he repeated somewhat sarcastically. "They don't really want to," said grandpa Joseph, "but their parents are pushing them into it."

Correspondence

To build confidence, your preparation for your speech will begin when you are first invited to speak. When invited in writing or by e-mail, you will have all the immediate contact details you need. Be careful, however, when making your arrangements by telephone, or face to face with your host. Having agreed a date, a subject, the venue and so forth, if you end your call or meeting without details of the brother inviting you to speak, you are courting disaster. There is always something, an afterthought that occurs or a summons is delayed, and all you can do is sit cross-fingered hoping that someone will have the good sense to be in touch with you one more time before the due date. Without lodge details you cannot even revert to the Registration Department of Grand Lodge who, under normal and justi-fiable circumstances, will gladly give you the personal details of a lodge secretary. Preparation for your speech will be much easier if you take pre-caution and ensure that you have all the particulars of your host from the start. Always request written confirmation of the agreed details for your talk and, where applicable, a copy of the summons to be sent to you in due course.

Summonses

The concept of being summoned, the demand from a higher authority for one's presence at a meeting or assembly, is embedded in antiquity. The operative stonemason had to conform to it, as required in the earliest rules

*Important
Tyler's Duties*
Lawson Wood
Postcard 1920s

and regulations of 1410, known as the *Cooke Manuscript*, which states that '. . . the Master and the Fellows before warned be come to such Congregation'. It is repeated by Anderson in our first *Constitutions of 1723* where the Charges of a Free-Mason includes the following: 'In ancient Times, no Master or Fellow could be absent from it (the lodge), especially when warn'd to appear at it, without incurring a severe Censure.' The summons plays a central part in our daily Masonic activities. It allows Metropolitan, Provincial or District Grand Lodges to keep an eye on every lodge under its jurisdiction. That watchful eye ensures that lodge secretaries issue summonses on time, but in the unlikely event that a formal summons fails to be issued, it would seem that the meeting, if held on the day named in the by-laws, is not a nullity. Any business, however, of which notice on the summons is required by the Book of Constitutions or the by-laws, cannot be lawfully transacted and must be deferred. It is certainly one aspect of the craft with which every Mason, from entered apprentice to Grand Master, is very familiar.

A summons may be seen as a lodge visiting card, and given the freedom of design, some wonderful depictions have appeared on modern summonses. In the early days, following the formation of the Premier Grand Lodge in 1717, the only decorative summonses were the ones issued by Grand Lodge demanding the presence of the Masters and Wardens of the various lodges to attend the regular Assemblies. Later ones incorporated delicately engraved detailed borders with various Masonic emblems. The ordinary lodge secretary summoned his members to meetings by the equivalent of a letter, distributed and delivered to each member by the Tyler of the lodge. Some early lodge minutes refer to the Tyler's activities in this regard. The Lodge of Antiquity in 1737 recorded in its minutes:

> 'Ordered that the Tyler for the future do deliver out the Summons for the meeting of this lodge, and be paid for the same One Shilling exclusively of his money for the Tyling.'

The Tyler's duties appear to have gradually extended to inserting items of business into the summons before delivery. The presence of Upper and Under Tylers in several lodges in the 1760s would suggest that his duties at the time extended well beyond the limited responsibilities of his modern counterpart. The Internet and e-mail facilities available today are a far cry from those early days. Nonetheless, we need to remain alert in this computerised environment and remember that where there is artificial intelligence, there must necessarily also be artificial stupidity:

> *I have a spelling checker;*
> *It came with my PC.*
> *It plainly marks four my revue*
> *Mistakes I cannot sea.*
> *I've run this poem threw it.*
> *I'm sure your pleased too no.*
> *It's letter perfect in it's weigh.*
> *My checker tolled me sew.*

'Spellbound' by Pennye Harper

The summons will serve many additional practical purposes which can assist you as a speaker. In addition to the exact details of the meeting and, importantly, as to what dress code you should note, it will also provide you with a list of names and ranks of the members. You may recognise a name or have the opportunity to comment on a well-known member or other. The summons of my mother lodge lists the names and addresses of all the members of the lodge.

6
When I was absent from home a whole night, arriving in the early hours of the morning, my darling Arimz asked where I had been and I told her the truth. The brethren of the lodge had a late night, more so than usual and

having ended the worse for wear, one of the brethren took me to his flat for the night. Unconvinced, my enterprising wife sent a circular to all 44 brethren listed on the summons enquiring as to whether I had spent the previous night in one of their homes. She received 44 replies, all saying 'yes'.

Visit the Venue

Having established the venue for your presentation, ensure that you are on site early, say, at least one hour before the proceedings. Should circumstances permit and the venue be in a location within a short distance and easy access, visit it a day or so before the evening of the event. This is quite easy on those occasions when you may be staying in the same premises or nearby overnight.

7

I was at the Ives Hotel in Glasgow, due to catch the 7.30am flight back to London after a successful speaking trip. On the last night out I was entertained royally and returned to the hotel late, past midnight. I asked the young lady at the reception desk for a 5.00am wake-up call and was astounded when she told me that I had to pay £10 for the call. "That is absolutely ridiculous," I protested. "A first class hotel, my room is costing me over £100, and you are going to bill me £10 for a wake-up call? Let me speak to the manager!" I demanded. Unfortunately it was too late at night. The manager had gone home and I had no option but to agree to the £10 charge for the call or no call was forthcoming. I went to bed nonplussed. Next morning I awoke to the ringing of the phone. A sweet voice said, "This is your 5.00am wake-up call, sir. And let me immediately say that we have waived the £10 charge for this call." I was relieved. "Thank you," I said. "What made you come to your senses?" I asked. "I am afraid it is now 9.00am," was the reply.

The purpose of a visit to the venue is to familiarise yourself with the surroundings and the preparations that may have already been made. It will avoid any surprises and you will have an advantage over your audience, which will add to your confidence. Ideally, the brother in charge of the evening's proceedings will be present. Otherwise make contact with the local caterer or hall manager, introducing yourself as the guest speaker.

8

Tony Blair, at the peak of his political career, was on a visit to an old ladies' home, shaking hands, smiling widely and making conversation with the octogenarians and asked a nonagenarian, "Do you know who I am, dear?" To which she replied, "I am sorry, I don't . . . But if you ask matron, she will be able to tell you."

Whoever is in charge will be able to inform you of the table plan. If you are fortunate, the room may already be set up and you will be able to identify your seat, normally at the top table. Stand by your seat and enjoy the sense of anticipation and the twinge of nervous electricity that will shoot through

Arriving At Your Function
Humphrey 1797 (Guildhall)

your system as you imagine the hall filled to the brim and all eyes turned on you. An early sense of nervousness is not only natural but also a good sign.

Acoustics and Microphones

Check the acoustics by speaking out loud to get a feel of the distance that your voice will carry in the room. Always avoid the use of a microphone if you possibly can. When there is no choice and you have to use one, you need to control that most disruptive action of turning your head away from the microphone whilst speaking. The resulting wave of your voice, rising and fading, is both distracting and most uncomfortable for the audience. The way to avoid this is by ensuring that you have a hand microphone available, rather than a fixed standing one. Rest the head of the microphone on the lower part of your chin, touching your skin so that when you turn your head, the microphone moves with you. When using this system, speak absolutely normally as you need not raise your voice or worry about the acoustics. Nonetheless, be sure you have the opportunity to test the microphone before you start speaking. When you address your audience without a microphone, which, I repeat, is the much-preferred method as it gives you total freedom of movement, keep in mind the fact that a crowded room absorbs the sound of your voice and you will not get the same echo as you would in an empty room. Projecting your voice becomes of paramount importance.

9
Ten minutes into my speech in an elongated and crowded room,
I asked, "Can everyone hear me?" "I can," replied a man in the front row,
"But I don't mind changing places with someone who can't."

Project your Voice

Projecting your voice is not as difficult as it may sound. The technical aspects of 'speaking from your stomach', extending your larynx, co-ordinating your breathing pattern and similar instructions, are intended for a prima donna and not for after-dinner speakers like you and me. To enable you to project your voice you need simple common sense and some practice. Make sure you speak loudly and clearly, enunciating each word deliberately and slowly. Look at the most distant member of your audience and be sure in your own mind that he or she can hear you. Always look ahead, not necessarily straight in front of you, but always in the direction in which you are speaking. Do not speak down, especially if glancing at your notes. Do not mumble. When hesitating, stop speaking or making any vocal sounds whilst you gather your thoughts and then start again, loudly and clearly. Do not hesitate to turn and face different sections of your audience. Be always conscious of those who are not within the immediate range of your vision.

Keep consistently on 'loud-mode'. Make a conscious effort to listen to the pitch of your voice, and if you sense that it is dropping, pick it up. Many speakers begin with a wonderful booming voice, which gradually fades after the first few moments to the consternation and disappointment of the audience. When not using a microphone, you cannot speak too loudly, short of shouting. Remember to find out how many people will be present in the audience.

10

On one occasion when I was late for the lecture I was due to give, I rushed into the room and headed straight to the speaker's podium to discover that only one person had remained. I apologised profusely and said, "There is no point in me delivering my speech just for you. Why don't we move to the bar and I will buy you a beer?" "I can't go," replied my new friend. "I am the next speaker."

Take note of the lighting, ensuring that any spotlights do not blind you. If you encounter any similar problems you can request that matters are put right for you there and then.

Observe your Surroundings

Here you have an opportunity to enhance your speech, even if already completed, with a few practical and topical observations. See how much you can find out about the building in which the meeting will take place. Through the 18th century, with the advent of nobility in our midst, some lodge meetings were held in the private homes and mansions of members of the aristocracy. The majority of lodges, however, continued to meet in taverns and a few coffee houses. The tavern of the period was an ideal venue for Freemasons, who met in an atmosphere of good fellowship, fun and happiness. The publican owner of the tavern was frequently made a Freemason, usually acting as the Tyler. Grand Lodge discouraged the practice. *The Engraved Lists of Lodges* published since 1723, leading to the current familiar *Year Book,* identified each lodge with a quaint copper engraved illustration of the tavern or coffee house sign where the lodge met. By the time Freemasonry began to spread at the end of the 17th century, the coffee house had been on the scene for well over a half-century. Yet Freemasons showed a preference for the tavern, probably because of the availability of alcohol, notwithstanding the more sophisticated atmosphere of the coffee house. Of the thirty lodges in London in 1726, only two met at a coffee house. In the next 150 years, some 400 new lodges were consecrated, only 34 of them in coffee houses.

Establishment of Masonic Halls

At the start of the 19th century, the establishment of Masonic halls and especially Freemasons' Hall at Great Queen Street in London, which incidentally, began its life as a tavern, changed the meeting habits of most lodges. Today, some lodges still meet in public houses, which are particularly popular with Schools and Lodges of Instruction. If you are an important venue, such as a City Club, Livery Hall or well-known Masonic hall, the room you are in will almost certainly have a name and the building an interesting history. The mother of all Livery Halls is the Mansion House, the home of the Lord Mayor of the City of London for the one-year that he or she holds that very high and prestigious office. A purpose-built home for the mayor was considered as early as 1666 following the Great Fire of London. It took another 70 years, however, to finally build the grandest of the surviving Georgian town palaces in London. Work began in 1739 and took 14 years and £70,000 to finish. The first Lord Mayor to use it was Sir Crispin Gascoigne who occupied the building in 1752 in spite of it not being completed. It is a lavish venue for banquets.

There are many hundreds of Freemasons among the 24,000 Liverymen in the City and twenty-one Livery Companies have their own Masonic lodges. There are also a number of City orientated Masonic lodges such as the City of London Installed Masters' Lodge and the City Livery Lodge, consisting exclusively of Liverymen whose Companies do not have their own Masonic lodge. Over the last century many Lord Mayors, Sheriffs, Aldermen, Common Councilmen and other city officials have been active Freemasons. The Guildhall Lodge number 3116 was specially consecrated in 1905 to cater for them. The City Livery lodges invariably dine in Livery Halls, which are all historical and outstanding venues, with catering of a particularly high standard. At the time of writing, just 40 halls provide accommodation for the 107 Livery Companies in the City of London.

Livery Halls

The Butchers' Company was chartered in 1561, though unlike many other Livery Companies in the City, it had no inherited endowments and almost all its assets are represented by its hall which was rebuilt after the Second World War. It is situated next to St Bartholomew's Hospital, and in 1983, extensive refurbishing took place with provision of an additional function room: the Taurus Suite in the lower ground floor, now often used as a Masonic temple. In 1996 major improvements were made to the building, in line with European Directives and Domestic legislation. Today, the Butchers' hall is a truly 21st century venue.

The Inn Holders, number 32 on the list of Liveries, was chartered in 1515. Close to the centre of the great fire, it was destroyed in 1666 with most of its early records. Fortunately, its fine silver and charters survived, because the Master was holding them in his home at the time. The hall was immediately rebuilt and completed in 1670. The earlier front doorway, the old courtroom and the magnificent dining hall have been barely altered since. The hall underwent radical repair in the 1880s and was again seriously damaged in the blitz of 1941. It had to be substantially restored between 1947 and 1952. Further improvement of facilities and the creation of a new entrance hall and reception room were completed in 1990. The venue, situated in College Street, is a very popular one.

Another of the smaller and quaint halls is that of the Worshipful Company of Bakers, number 19 on the list of Liveries, chartered in 1486. The hall, hidden away in Harp Lane near the Tower of London, is the fourth one on the original freehold site of 1506. It was built in 1963 and was financed by the construction of a modern block of offices above the Company's premises. In 1490, the Bakers hired a tenement in Dowgate for £3 a year, and in 1506 they purchased their first proper hall for £20, a large mansion in Sigrymes Lane now named Harp Lane. The Mansion was lost in the Great Fire of London. Sadly, in 1715, a similar fate befell the second hall, which had wisely been insured for £750. The third hall, which was completed in 1722, survived for over 200 years but was destroyed on the night of the first blitz on 29 December 1940. An interesting relic from this hall is the old oak 'Charter Box' dated 1722, now in the anteroom of the new hall. Also saved is the Beadle's oak seat in the vestibule and a set of eight large marble panels executed in 1882 that line the walls of the staircase depicting the life of the Company through the ages.

These are just three instances selected at random that represent the background and fascinating history behind the Livery Halls in the city. When contacting a Livery Hall, you will find that the man in charge is the Beadle, the equivalent to the hall manager. He will give you firsthand details and relevant literature describing the venue which you can then embellish, if need be, with information from your library and the Internet.

Deviating from Livery Halls, many formal occasions in London are held in the stupendous Inns of Court of which the Middle Temple Hall is probably the most spectacular. The first hall on this site was built in 1302, the present one completed in 1573, and it is thought that William Shakespeare attended the opening night of his play 'Twelfth Night' here on 2 February 1601. The inside of the hall, where dinners have been held since the 14th century, has an outstanding double hammer beam oak roof. A twenty-nine-foot table at the end of the hall, known as the Bench Table, is made from a single oak tree and was a gift from Queen Elizabeth I. Beyond it is The Cupboard around which the well-known moots, or legal debate rehearsals, take place. On the west wall hang royal portraits, and around the entire hall, a spectacular array of Elizabethan suits of armour. Famous names are associated with the hall: John Evelyn, Thomas More, Charles Dickens, Sir Francis Drake, Sir Walter Raleigh and Elias Ashmole, among many others, who were members of the very select Honourable Society of the Middle Temple, which has flourished for six centuries or more.

Whichever venue you are visiting, small or big, modest or opulent, even the street through which you entered the building can be usefully integrated into your speech to serve as an excellent start or ending. Before leaving the room in which you will be speaking, look around you one more time – anything unusual or of interest in the room? Are there any tapestries, particular paintings or portraits on the walls? If so, obtain the details from the plaque on the painting or enquire from the helpful Beadle or hall manager. A speech that starts, "Ladies and gentlemen, very much aware of being under the stern gaze of Bro Christopher Wren on my right," will immediately focus the attention of your audience and has all the promise of being interesting. Remember you are not an expert and do not pretend to possess excessive understanding of a subject with which you are not particularly familiar.

11

One Saturday morning in the Camden Passage Antique Market in London, where I have been a long-standing visitor (as well as a tenant for some 22 years), I noticed a street vendor with a row of mediocre paintings leaning against the railings. As I walked past, I glanced at the paintings and suddenly froze. There among the insignificant and worn paintings was an original Van Gogh. Incredible as the circumstances were, I had no doubts whatsoever that it was an original. I looked at the vendor. He was crouching on his knees, unshaven in a worn T-shirt and sandals, the end of a spent cigarette hanging from the side of his mouth. This man could not have been mistaken for an expert by any stretch of the imagination. As nonchalantly as I could, I picked one of the other paintings and casually enquired, "How much for this one, please?" The vendor slowly stood to his feet, reached into the back pocket of his torn jeans and drew out a soiled sheet of paper. "What's the number of the back?" he asked. "Number 12," I replied, my heartbeat increasing with anticipation. "No 12 . . ." said the vendor going down his list. "That is 10 quid, mate." "How about No 9?" I asked, picking up another of the inconsequential paintings. "No 9 is 15 pounds," was the reply. I went for the big one. I picked up the original Van Gogh by the corner of the broken frame. Lifting it high with two fingers and away from him, I said, "How about No 21?" "No 21?" repeated the seller as he went down the list. "No 21 is one and a half million."

Dress Code

As the guest speaker you will be on show, so to speak, all the time. From the moment you make yourself known to your host, you will be introduced as the guest of honour, or the speaker for the evening, and every move and action you make will be observed. As you improve as a speaker, you will find the range of invitations extending beyond Freemasonry. On each occasion, whether at a formal banquet or a Women's Institute gathering, the norm will be the same. When you stand up to speak everybody's gaze is upon you. You need to look smart. The better you look the more confident you will feel. First and foremost, be sure you are wearing the correct dress code. You will feel uncomfortable wearing a bright yellow and red tie and blue shirt surrounded by an audience in dinner jackets. You could get away with the opposite – wearing a dinner jacket as a guest speaker at an informal meeting, but why embarrass your hosts by overdressing? If in doubt, check with your host and get it right. At Masonic functions, the most common dress code, usually stated on the summons, will read as follows or will be a close variation of: 'dark suit, white gloves, undress regalia, black or craft tie'. Sometimes, especially at installation or anniversary meetings, the summons will require you to wear a black tie, namely a dinner jacket. In some instances this may apply to the Officers of the lodge only, and on such occasions you have the option to do so, if you wish. As the guest speaker, it is recommended that you do.

Full Dress

When attending lodge meetings preceding the function you are invited to speak at, take note of the occasions when full dress regalia is required. Whilst every lodge has the prerogative to request that full regalia be worn, Rule 257 dictates the standard practice in our book of *Constitutions*. It essentially states that, *unless impracticable,* full regalia is worn in Grand Lodge, at special occasions such as consecrations or anniversaries, or at a Metropolitan, District or Provincial Grand Lodge, when so required. As a courtesy, a Grand Officer will comply with the request of a private lodge to wear full regalia. Provincial and Metropolitan Grand Officers and London and Senior London Grand Rank are expected to follow whatever instructions apply to Grand Officers, although far more leeway is given to individual brethren with Provincial rank, to wear the regalia they find most convenient. Do note the difference between Grand Officers and Grand

Proper
Masonic Dress
USA Are You a Mason?
postcard series 1920s

Lodge Officers which, whilst not a formal differentiation, implies a Past rank in the first instance and an Active or Present rank in the latter. Active or Present rank officers of the Grand Lodge are entitled to wear a chain on the official occasions referred to above.

Today's requirement to be dressed in a black suit, white shirt and black or Masonic tie is informal compared to Victorian times, which extended well into the 20th century. In London, evening dress, what is now referred to as black tie, was often obligatory at lodge meetings. In Provincial lodges evening dress was reserved for the installation meeting and consisted of the standard swallowtail coat, black cutaway waistcoat, black trousers and tie, which was in fashion in the 1860s. Masons in the armed forces wore their uniform and would have looked smart with their aprons and collars over a stiff white shirt and a short scarlet jacket.

Ties

Ties have long served as an effective way of highlighting an organisation's identity and they do give a sense of membership and belonging to a club or society. When ties were first worn in about the middle of the 19th century they were large, floppy and of various colours. The norm for the lodge was a white bow tie.

12

My sweet mum gave me two beautiful and colourful ties for New Year. At dinner that very evening, I proudly wore the bright red polka dot one and approached my mum for a thank you hug when she looked straight at me and said, "Why are you wearing the red tie? Didn't you like the blue one I gave you?"

It would appear that there is no suggestion in the 19th century that the tie worn in lodge with formal morning dress or a lounge suit should be black. It is a custom originally associated with the wearing of the black silk bow tie when dinner jackets came into fashion in the mid-19th century. After the First World War, it became standard practice by Freemasons to wear a black tie in memory of the brethren who had perished while serving in the forces. Today's regulation regarding ties is laid out in the *Information for the Guidance of Members of the Craft* which establishes the Craft tie as official and allows the option to wear Craft or black ties at meetings. The special design of the official Craft tie is a copyright of Grand Lodge manufactured by Toye, Kenning and Spencer Ltd. It is available exclusively from Letchworth's, the shop in Grand Lodge. Otherwise, several regalia manufacturers have come up with alternative similar-looking designs, none of which is acceptable as a substitute.

Outside Freemasonry, dress codes are not that simple. Bearing in mind Oscar Wilde's immortal comment 'it is only shallow people who do not judge by appearances', let me briefly guide you through the intricate world of proper dress codes. George Bryan Brummell (1778-1840), the English dandy and wit known as Beau Brummell, is often credited with the invention of the formal suit during the early 19th century. He appeared at formal functions dressed in black and white when more colourful attire was the standard dress. He was much admired for his fastidious appearance. As he was close to the Prince of Wales, later King George IV, Brummell was an influence on fashion of the day and men of society imitated his style. By the time he was estranged from the Prince of Wales and his influence subsided, he had set the fashion for trousers rather than breeches, dark, simply cut clothes and elaborate neckwear. In debt from gambling, Brummell fled to France in 1816, and lived in poverty and squalor, dying in an asylum for the insane in Caen on 30 March 1840.

13
    Business was at its lowest ebb for my colleague Grimsby, who for a very long time had been struggling and borrowing in an attempt to avoid bankruptcy. His philosophy is reflected in his own words when he once said to me, "I intend to live within my income even if I have to borrow to do so." Out of the blue, good fortune struck and he won no less than one million pounds in the National Lottery. In the press interview that followed the reception celebrating his success, a reporter asked him what he was going to do with the money. Grimsby responded without the slightest hesitation. "The first thing," replied Grimsby, "I am going to do is pay off my ten creditors." "What about the rest?" asked the same reporter. "The rest?" replied Grimsby. "I am afraid the rest will have to wait!"

Black Tie

The most common requirement for formal evenings is the black tie, commonly referred to as the tuxedo in the USA. This is a dinner jacket with black bow tie. It is the required attire on those occasions when the event is not formal enough to require the white tie. The dinner jacket originated as a less formal dress than the constricting swallowtail evening coat and bone-hard white bow tie of the mid-19th century. It was meant for use at home and in the privacy of well-established London clubs. The creation of the first design of a dinner jacket is attributed to Henry Poole & Co of Savile Row who claimed to have made a short smoking jacket for the Prince of Wales, later King Edward VII, in 1865. The prince wore the dinner jacket with a black bow tie, and quite naturally, the fashion was copied, first by gentlemen in his entourage, soon expanding beyond royal circles.

    The waist sash, called a cummerbund, originated after the First World War from military dress in British India. When required to wear the black tie, there are accompanying conventions from which some leeway is allowed. The requisite black silk bow tie may be of any other colour but white and still qualify. The jacket, a short black coat with silk lapels, may be single or double-breasted. When wearing a single- breasted jacket, it would be incorrect to have more than one button and it is common to also wear either a black waistcoat which should be low-cut and made of the same material as the lapels of the jacket, or a cummerbund worn with the pleats facing up, but not both. The black trousers will have a single row of silk braid down each leg. The trousers do not have turn-ups or belt loops as it is customary to wear them with braces. The shirt must be a white plain-fronted dress shirt with a Marcella cotton front. Socks must be black, worn with black leather shoes.

14
    My daughter Anad would have only been about eight years old when I had been regularly attending a series of formal functions. As I was dressing

for yet another city event, she watched in silence for a while. "Daddy, you shouldn't wear that black tie," she finally said looking concerned. "And why not, darling?" I asked. "Because you know that it always gives you a headache the next morning," she replied.

White Tie

White tie or full evening dress is the most formal dress code that exists for civilians today in the United Kingdom. It is worn on formal state occasions, even when such occasions, for instance, the State Opening of Parliament, occur during the day. Formal evening dress ie, the white tie, is more strictly regulated than other forms of dress. It consists of an evening tailcoat, trousers, white shirt, white waistcoat and white bow tie. The black tailcoat with silk facings is sharply cutaway at the front. Trousers are black with two lines of braid. A white stiff-fronted shirt is worn with silver or white cuff links and a white stiff wing collar, attached to the shirt with silver or white collar studs. The waistcoat is white and low-cut. Black silk stockings should be worn with black patent leather pumps or shoes. The Lord Mayor and Sheriffs of the City of London will wear knee-breeches, silk stockings and black buckled pumps instead of trousers at the Mansion House banquets, famously snubbed by Gordon Brown some years ago, who chose to ignore the dress code thus making headlines.

Be careful when you receive an invitation giving you instructions for the required dress code. The black and white tie dress are relatively straight-forward but there are umpteen other terms that may appear on a formal or semi-formal invitation: day formal for diplomatic receptions; evening formal for the opera or a charity ball; cocktail attire, business attire, sports attire, among many more. Your host may not say what he or she means and you, especially if a guest of honour, still have to get it right. Do not hesitate to clarify with your host the exact dress intended for the evening. The final 'code', the bottom line, is to look clean-cut and well dressed for the occasion. Do not forget to have a haircut.

15
   I found myself in the embarrassing situation, having obviously exceeded the allotted time for my speech, of having a member of the audience stand up to walk out of the hall. "Excuse me, where are you going, sir?" I demanded, naturally irritated by his interruption and disturbance. "I am going to have a haircut," he replied. "A haircut?" I exclaimed incredulously. "Couldn't you have had a haircut before I started speaking?" "Before you started speaking, I did not need a haircut."

Your partner

As a guest speaker, as often as not, you will be invited to bring your partner with you. Some formal rules apply to your lady partner when you are wearing formal dress. If you wear black tie, the corresponding female attire can range from a short cocktail dress to a long gown, depending on fashion, local custom and the hour at which the function takes place. When you attend a white tie function, your lady must wear a formal ball gown with her best accessories and jewellery. If decorations are specified in the invitation, married women may wear tiaras. On less formal occasions ensure that an invitation extended to your partner is not a mere 'polite' one, for instance, where you are the only one invited to have your partner with you. If in doubt, enquire as to the acceptability and suitability of your partner's presence. Should you wish to take the initiative in asking to have your partner, or a friend or colleague accompany you, do offer to pay for their dinner. You will almost invariably be seated together at the top table or its equivalent and it is as essential for your partner to look the part as it is for you.

You are now ready to join the party.

---

16 Contempt of Court

When I became a lawyer, I distinctly remember being advised never to ask a witness a question if I was not prepared for all possible answers. The example given to emphasise the advice, referred to a trial in a small town where the prosecuting attorney called his first witness to the stand. The witness was an elderly grandmother. The lawyer approached her and asked, "Mrs Jones, do you know me?" "Why yes, I do know you, Mr Williams," she responded. "I have known you since you were a young boy, and frankly, you have been a big disappointment to me. You lie, you cheat on your wife, you manipulate people and talk about them behind their backs. You think you're a big shot when you haven't the brains to realise that you will never amount to anything more than a two-bit paper pusher lawyer. Yes, Mr Williams, I know you." The lawyer was stunned. Not knowing what to say, he pointed across the room and asked, "Mrs Jones, do you know the defence attorney?" She again replied, "Why yes, I've known Mr Bradley since he was a youngster, too. He's lazy, bigoted and he has a drinking problem. He can't build a normal relationship with anyone and his law practice is one of the worst in the country. Not to mention he cheated on his wife with three different women. One of them was your wife, Mr Williams. Yes, I know him, too." The defence attorney turned purple with embarrassment. At this stage the judge asked both counsellors to approach the bench and in a very quiet voice said, "If either of you asks her if she knows me, I'll throw you in jail for contempt of court."

17 Money

I received the following thought provoking text from Afolabi in Ghana, with whom I had developed a close relationship by correspondence over a period of several years. I am still trying to determine how serious he was:

Money, it can buy a house, but not a home
It can buy a clock, but not time
It can buy you a position, but not respect
It can buy you a bed, but not sleep

It can buy you a book, but not knowledge
It can buy you medicine, but not health
It can buy you blood, but not life
So you see money isn't everything, and it often causes pain
and suffering. I am telling you this because I am your friend,
and as your friend I want to take away your pain and suffering
. . . So why don't you send me all your money and I will suffer for you
Cash only please! After all, what are friends for, huh?

18 Music to the Ears

Bernard intensely disliked visiting his bank manager. It was always a hassle and troublesome. On Monday 15 February, he went in for his monthly meeting when the clerk said to him, "I am very sorry to have to inform you that Mr Smith, our manager, died over the weekend." Bernard expressed his condolences and walked out to return the next day. "Can I speak with Mr Smith, the bank manager, please?" he asked. It was the same clerk who responded, "But you were here yesterday. We told you that Mr Smith died on the golf course over the weekend. His funeral will be taking place on Wednesday next week." Bernard nodded, "Oh yes, thank you," and walked out again. He was back on the Wednesday. "Is Mr Smith here please?" he asked. "I don't understand," said the exasperated clerk. "This is the third day you are in here. We have told you quite categorically, Mr Smith, the bank manager, is dead. Why do you keep asking?" "Because it is like music to my ears," replied Bernard.

19 Washington Post Competition

The following entries were the recent winners in the Washington Post yearly contest for alternative meanings to various English words:

1. *Coffee (n.), a person who is coughed upon.*
2. *Flabbergasted (adj.), appalled over how much weight you have gained.*
3. *Abdicate (v.), to give up all hope of ever having a flat stomach.*
4. *Esplanade (v.), to attempt an explanation while drunk.*
5. *Willy-nilly (adj.), impotent.*
6. *Negligent (adj.), describes a condition in which you absent-mindedly answer the door in your nightgown.*
7. *Lymph (v), to walk with a lisp.*
8. *Gargoyle (n.), an olive-flavoured mouthwash.*
9. *Flatulence (n.), the emergency vehicle that picks you up after you are run over by a steamroller.*
10. *Testicle (n.), a humorous question in an exam.*
11. *Rectitude (n.), the formal, dignified demeanour assumed by a proctologist immediately before he examines you.*
12. *Oyster (n.), a person who sprinkles his conversation with Yiddish expressions.*
13. *Pokemon (n), a Jamaican proctologist.*
14. *Frisbeetarianism (n.), the belief that when you die, your soul goes up on the roof and gets stuck there.*
15. *Circumvent (n.), the opening in the front of boxer shorts.*

Chapter 1 summary

- You cannot be too well prepared as a speaker
- Request written confirmation of the invitation
- Be on site early
- Learn something about the venue
- Check the acoustics, lighting etc
- Observe your surroundings
- Look smart and use correct dress code
- Ensure your partner matches you

Chapter 1 anecdotes

1   *Prepare to be Spontaneous* (Introduction)
2   *Money in your Pocket* (Introduction)
3   *Guns for the Inviter*
4   *Can Still Hear Him Speak*
5   *Granddad's Insurance*
6   *Responses to Summons*
7   *Wake-up Call*
8   *Matron Will Tell You*
9   *Can Everyone Hear Me?*
10   *I am the Next Speaker*
11   *Original Van Gogh*
12   *Two Gift Ties*
13   *The Rest Will Have To Wait*
14   *Morning Headache*
15   *Going To Have a Haircut*

Chapter 1 additional anecdotes

16   *Contempt of Court*
17   *Money*
18   *Music to the Ears*
19   *Washington Post Competition*

Hors d'œuvres:
At dinner

1723 and all that

The first book of *Constitutions* was published by James Anderson in April 1723. Was it a curse or a blessing? After all, for six previous years since June 1717, Freemasons were doing pretty well, regularly meeting at taverns, dining and drinking whilst learning the ritual and conducting the ceremonies. For those first six years of organised Freemasonry there were no rules or regulations, no Grand Secretary or Grand Chancellor looking after Masonic affairs, no attendance books and no minutes kept. Six happy years and all seemed to be fine and dandy. So who was the spoilsport who put an end to pure pleasure and fun and decided that the Society needed numerated guidelines for its conduct and comportment? The answer: it was the Reverend John Theophilus Desaguliers (1683-1744), the third Grand Master of whom a great deal is known as a scientist and gentleman, but next to nothing of his Masonic career prior to 1719. That is not surprising, however, when considering that Desaguliers chose to become a Freemason just to check the fraternity out and to discover if any of the supposed secrets had a hermetic, esoteric or mystic significance.

His daily activity at the time, with his fellow colleagues in the Royal Society of which he was curator, was spent on the study of experimental philosophy searching, in simplistic terms, for that one secret in nature that may answer a hundred questions. Could Freemasons have something in their 'secrets' that could be significant? As unlikely as that may have been, it needed checking out. John Desaguliers went through the ceremony of initiation and a little more, in order to discover that the secrets were inconsequential – nothing more than signs and words leading from one degree to the next – and nothing to talk about. His curiosity and concerns satisfied, he was impressed by the genuine love, relief and truth practised in the lodge room. He returned to his friends and colleagues and, true to his obligation, denied them any knowledge he had attained in lodge. On the contrary, he encouraged them to join the fraternity to enjoy the experience he had recently gone through. It was important, however, that in order to secure the participation of such prominent men, the aristocracy and even royalty, the society of Freemasons would have to organise itself into some order. What better way than a book of rules? As early as 1719, as he was on the verge of being appointed Grand Master, Desaguliers *charged* James Anderson to *digest* the ancient constitutions of the operative Masons and come up with the rules and regulations: the *Constitutions of 1723* (don't ask why in the plural – nobody knows). They have guided us ever since.

Observe your Audience

Your observations of your surroundings mentioned in the previous chapter should extend to your audience. The advantage of being among the first to arrive at the venue is the opportunity to observe and evaluate the guests as they enter the room. It is quite natural to feel relaxed when surrounded by friends and colleagues. You are less likely to feel nervous or concerned when you stand in lodge to comment or even give a short talk to the brethren whose familiar faces surround you. It is a different story when addressing a hall full of strangers. If you let your imagination take over, you may well spot faces that appear antagonistic and troublesome. This will not happen if you familiarise yourself with the audience. Keep an open mind and observe as many of the members of your audience as you can. Listen rather than talk, making mental notes of comments and let your confidence grow as more and more of the individuals you speak to become familiar faces: later, you will recognise them in the audience. Table arrangements and 'who sits where' is not your concern. Never be tempted to change nameplates on the table, and take your place as instructed.

20
Four ladies, close bridge friends who had spent a great deal of time together, found the conversation at dinner reaching a highly intimate level. "I feel so close to you three," said one, "that I will admit for the very first time, in absolute confidence, that I have been a kleptomaniac for most of my life." A few minutes of stunned silence followed and another of the friends said, "Well, if you have the courage to be so honest, I will tell you, because I trust you all, that nobody but nobody – not even my husband – knows that I am a practising nymphomaniac." More stunned silence and the third lady volunteered that her sense of guilt over the abuse of her children was ruining her marriage and life. It was the turn of the fourth friend. As they turned to face her she meekly commented, "I only have one irrepressible weakness . . . an urge to gossip."

Behaviour

Needless to say, whilst under observation by all and sundry, your behaviour – beyond natural motion and gestures – needs to be impeccable. Do not fidget with objects on the table and do not scratch yourself on any part of your body. Do not speak too loudly (except when on your feet giving your talk), in fact, I repeat, do the listening rather than the talking. Do not immerse yourself in conversation just with your partner. Feel comfortable in yourself and those around you will feel comfortable with you. Whenever

I open my mouth, in any one of the six languages I speak by force of circumstance, the question of my accent comes up. I need to explain that whilst I was born in Turkey, from a Russian father and Greek mother, I have Israeli nationality, although I am a very proud British citizen. I went to school in Italy and spent a major part of my working life in South America. Thus, whilst a little confused, I still speak several languages reasonably fluently. On the other hand, I had a colleague who spoke a dozen languages . . . all of them in English.

My wife Arimz, who was my sergeant in the Israeli Defence Forces, admits to having Welsh blood in her veins on her paternal side.

21
Not long ago we decided to visit her ancestral village of Pontrhydfendigaid in Ceredigion, on the River Teifi. The village name remains unpronounceable to us to this day. After the lengthy car journey, we were delighted to enter the village and stopped at the first eating establishment we could find. When approached by a pretty waitress for our order, I said, "Would you please pronounce for us, very slowly, exactly where we are?" The young lady leaned forward and in an impeccable Welsh accent drawled, "Buuur . . . geeeer . . . Kiiiiing."

22
On our return, I was enthusing about the outstanding Welsh countryside when the Master of my lodge, to my surprise, commented, "Wales?" he said. "That country is famous for only two things: harlots and rugby players!" I was taken aback. "How can you make such a comment, David?" I asked, somewhat offended. "You may not know it but my wife is Welsh." "Really?" David replied without a moment's hesitation. "What position does she play?"

Name Badges

Should you be given a name badge, first check that your name is correctly spelled. Be sure to place it on your lapel or above your top jacket pocket at a height convenient for those facing you to read. See that it is easily legible and not hidden by your lapel or pocket-handkerchief. Do not hesitate to be seen to be reading the names of those you are speaking to. You need not make any special effort to remember the names you come across – it is your enemies you have to remember well, the names of friends you can afford to forget.

23
At a plush reception I was delighted to be reintroduced to a gentleman I recalled well, having memorised his name by association. In an effort to impress him, I greeted him before he was introduced: "It is good to meet you again, Mr Horror," I said. "My name is *Münster*," came the curt reply. I could have made the same mistake, I suppose, with Mr Hamburg and Mr Frankfurt.

Food and Drink

Avoid alcohol before you speak. This is important for two reasons: first you may accidentally exceed that happy state of mind that so easily translates from jollity to ridicule. We can all control ourselves with just one drink and no more, but why take the risk?

24
As a man of habit I always stay at the same hotel in any one city. One time, I was at the Grand Hotel in Manchester on an almost weekly basis for several months. On the first evening at the bar I heard a man sitting next to me order two single whiskies and down them separately. When he did the same for a third time, my curiosity was aroused. "Why not a double whisky?" I asked. "Is this some superstition?" "Not at all," replied my new friend Patrick. "You see, after the war, my dearest and closest colleague in arms, Nelson, went off to Canada and I came to England and we agreed always to drink separate whiskies and recall our great friendship," he explained. Thus for several weeks, on each visit to the Grand, the two of us downed three whiskies at a time between us and exchanged great yarns of wartime adventures and drank to the health of Nelson. One Saturday I turned up at the Grand and there was Patrick sitting at the bar with one single whisky in front of him. My heart sank. I approached him, placed a consoling hand on his shoulder and said "Nelson is dead, isn't he?" "Oh no!" replied Patrick. "It is me that's given up drinking."

At formal receptions and dinners a glass of whisky may well be beyond the controlled measure of a pub or bar. Here the waiters will be refilling your wine glass repeatedly as you sip away unaware. The dangers are all there. It is not worth the risk. Being a teetotaller for a couple of hours has its compensations: first, the taste of the wine *after* your speech will be twice as delicious. Secondly, and more importantly, you may find that, no matter how far you deny it, your apparent reliance on a "small" drink before a speech becomes a cumbersome inconvenience. This consideration has to be put in context as it is entirely psychological, nonetheless a genuine threat to a speaker. You may find early in your speaking career that a shot of whisky or a glass of wine steadies your nerves and 'oils' your tongue. Be aware of this great danger. You will be getting into a habit that will not serve you well. The times when you are unable to obtain a drink, no matter how obviously unnecessary for the occasion, you will be unsteadied beyond need. Audiences are far more aware and sensitive than you think. You may feel that you are less nervous and better prepared with a small quantity of alcohol in your system but you will not project that feeling to an astute audience. I repeat, don't risk it. Don't drink.

25
Winston Churchill, at a dinner reception, tasted the whisky handed to him and with a derisive look asked the waiter whether he had poured the

whisky or the water first into the glass. "The whisky," replied the disconcerted waiter. "Then I should be reaching it any moment now, shouldn't I?" was Winston's sardonic comment.

26
I myself find that I have an inclination to get drunk after just one drink . . . usually the fifteenth.

27
In the Grand Hotel in Manchester, spending another night on Masonic business, I found a copy of the Bible on the side table and instinctively opened the cover. On the margin, in bold letters, a sentence read: If you have opened this Bible because you are an alcoholic please ring 0161 881 1638. My curiosity aroused, I dialled the number. I was astounded to be welcomed by a coarse voice that said, "Good evening. Premier Off-Licence and Wine Merchants, can I help you?"

Much of what has been said about alcohol applies, to a lesser extent, also to food. Plentiful delicious hors d'œuvres followed by a full five-course meal, including dessert and cheese, is not the ideal preparation for after-dinner speaking. The need for digestion will slow your metabolism and drain your brain of blood – you need to remain sharp and alert. Eat sensibly avoiding preliminary peanuts, crisps and snacks. Eat lightly by requesting small portions from the waiter serving you and be careful you do not give offence by leaving food on your plate. Do not drink coffee if you have a weak bladder.

28
On a visit to Beijing in China, with a small group of American friends, we were returning to our hotel late at night when we lost our way. Unable to hold back, we finally stood against a wall about to relieve ourselves when a Chinese gentleman tapped my American friend on the shoulder. He signalled us to follow him. We found ourselves in a beautiful garden, surrounded by trees and flowers. The Chinese gentleman signalled us to proceed with what we were about to do. Thanking him with a bow of the head, I said, "Thank you for this Chinese courtesy," to which he replied, "This not Chinese courtesy . . . this American Embassy!"

Conversation

On the day of your speech make sure you are *au fait* with the day's news. Go through the headlines of the daily newspaper, if you are not a regular daily newsreader. It will serve you well at the reception and dinner conversation. Whilst you will do better by listening than talking, you will be expected to comment about yourself to an audience that will naturally be curious about their speaker. Answer the questions that will repeatedly be asked of you, with brief and exact replies. You will invariably be asked personal questions. Do not hesitate and make those surrounding you feel that they are welcome to have an insight into your life. Be modest and be brief. Having replied to the usual enquiries of your place of birth or unusual accent, turn the same question round and ask it of your enquirer. The most topical subject for any speech is an occurrence during the course of that same evening's events – something or someone that is familiar to the whole audience. The more personal the comment, the greater the effect it will have and it works best when the subject is someone prominent in the evening's proceedings, such as the Chairman, President or even the Toast Master. Make sure that you have the tacit or overt approval of the person concerned. This is usually a matter of judgement. If uncertain, simply approach and ask him or her whether you may mention them in your speech in a light-hearted context. Ensure you do not offend or appear to be breaching a confidence.

29

At a formal ambassadorial dinner, I sat next to a Japanese gentleman who was intently staring at his soup. "Nicey soupy?" I enquired in what I felt was as near as I could possibly get to the language. I was totally ignored. When the next dish was laid before him and my neighbour again made no gesture beyond concentrating on his food, I tried one more time to make polite conversation. "Fishy goodie?" I asked. I gave up when there was no response whatsoever. You may imagine my embarrassment at the end of the meal when my Japanese colleague stood up to give the key speech of the evening, which he did in perfect Oxford English. When he sat down, he turned to me and said, "Likey speechey?" He did apologise and explained that he was concentrating on his speech and did not want to be distracted.

Ceremonies and Procedures

Different occasions call for different procedures and it is well worthwhile to enquire if any special ceremony will take place at the festive board or the dinner you are attending. Grace is standard:

> 'For what we are about to receive may the Great
> Architect of the Universe give us grateful hearts and
> keep us mindful of the needs of others.'

Grace is usually given by the Chaplain in a lodge or a man of the cloth, when present, in other meetings. At times, the grace is sung. There are many deviations and versions and there is no rule governing the content or delivery of a grace. One Latin grace will be familiar to Royal Arch Masons: *Benedictus Benedicat* which translates as 'May the Blessed One Bless'. At the end of the meal the grace given is *Benedicto Benedicatur*, namely 'May the Blessed One be Blessed'.

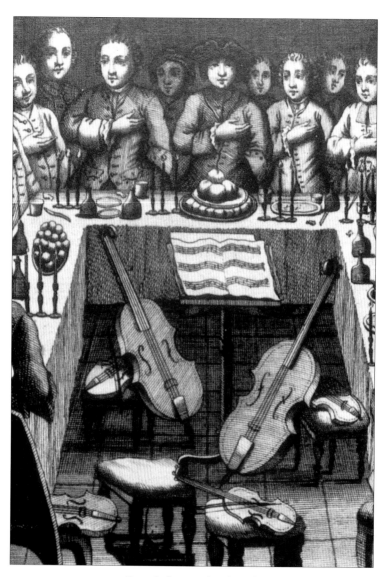

Grace before meal and music
French print c1790

30
An easy one to remember, should you be asked to say grace by surprise before or after a meal, is the shortest grace on record: 'Pa, Ta – Amen'. It must be said with respect notwithstanding the amusing content. Timing and gestures on this occasion are crucial. Raise your head towards heaven as you utter, even intone, the word 'Pa'. Pause and look back down onto your plate on the table as you say 'Ta' in the same tone. Finally look at those sharing the meal and then state 'Amen'.

31
The Bishop of Southwark found himself having an agreeable time at a reception for a dinner party, enjoying a third or fourth glass of sherry, surrounded by flirty young ladies fascinated by his demeanour and insisting on sitting with him at dinner. When the evening's proceedings were about to start the President called on the Bishop to give grace, which the Bishop, to the surprise of all present, refused to do. When approached later as to the reason for his refusal, he explained: "I rarely refuse to bless the food we are about to eat. On this occasion, however, I felt it was not quite the right time for me to attract God's attention to my circumstances."

Masonic Fire

Drinking to the health of the Sovereign, the Grand Master and other toasts is standard procedure. In the instance of Masonic Fire different provinces vary the pattern and speed of the fire. Your hosts would see it as a compliment and respect for their traditions if you familiarise yourself with their fire and execute it correctly at the appropriate time. The fire, which appears to be an exclusive Masonic practice, is given at the culmination of a toast and intended to honour the recipient. The origins of the fire are military. There are exact records of Sir John Peake, Lord Mayor of the City of London in 1686, visiting each of the City Gates to toast the King and Queen and local residents of the respective Wards. Following each toast, the military guard who accompanied him on these *tours de force,* fired a volley from their muskets. The symbolic adoption of this practice by Freemasons is recorded in 18th century exposures. The festive board is described with brethren sitting around a table, each with a bottle of wine which is referred to as the Barrel. The wine is Red Powder and the water White Powder whilst the drinking goblets are called Cannons. The military allusions continue in the proceedings: following the toast to the Monarch, the Worshipful Master instructs the brethren to 'take powder', that is to fill their glasses. (The modern equivalent we use is 'charge your glasses', which maintains the military connotation.) This is followed by 'present arms', ie raise your glasses, 'take aim', by which the full wine glass is brought to the lips, and finally 'fire': drink. To quote the exposure verbatim: 'All watching the Master all of the time and all being done in military fashion – with perfect disciplined unison. The Master then says "good-fire" at which time the goblets, in perfect timing are banged with force and noise on the table followed by three claps and three times the loud cry "VIVAT" or "HUZZA".' Since 1741, when the above was first published, there have been variations and many refinements to the procedure.

The Loving Cup

There are other ceremonies that can be more elaborate which need to be practised to avoid embarrassment, especially when you are the primary guest and may even be expected to commence the proceedings. The ceremony of drinking from the Loving Cup is such an example, and is a standard procedure at Livery Banquets and periodically witnessed at Masonic gatherings. In principle, the procedure deviates a little at each function but is essentially the same: immediately after the dinner and grace, the Master and Wardens drink a hearty welcome to their guests from the Loving Cup. This is a three-handled silver or silver-gilt receptacle filled with spiced wine known by the old English term 'Sack'. The Cup is then passed round the table, usually to the left. Each guest in turn stands up to pledge to his neighbour with the Loving Cup. They bow to each other (a bow in City and Masonic circles is given by an inclination of the head only, body erect) and the guest to their left removes the cover of the Cup with their right hand, holding it at shoulder-height for all to see, whilst his colleague drinks.

When finished drinking, he applies the napkin, which is appended to one of the handles, to the lip of the Cup. The lid is then replaced, they bow again, the Cup held by them both is passed, always clasped with both hands, to the guest who held the lid. He rotates left to face his neighbour, and the guest who finished drinking remains standing behind him looking outwards, thus protecting the drinker's back. The procedure is repeated as the Loving Cup is thus shared and passed from guest to guest. The commonly accepted source for the ceremony traces its roots to the assassination of Edward the Martyr at Corfe Castle by his stepmother Elfrida in 978 AD, while drinking from a cup she presented him. It was customary at drinking parties in Anglo Saxon times to pass round a large cup or drinking horn, from which each drank in turn whilst standing to honour the company present. As he lifted the cup with both hands, the drinker was exposed and vulnerable to his enemies who may have wished to kill him. Thus a tradition developed whereby a drinker required the companion who sat next to him to be his pledge. If he consented, his companion stood up and raised his drawn sword to protect the drinker.

32
I attended the Mansion House dinner hosted by the Lord Mayor, at which the Turkish Ambassador was the guest of honour. My Lord Mayor, who knew of my Turkish origins, asked that I explain to the Ambassador the procedure for drinking from the Loving Cup as described above and I did so

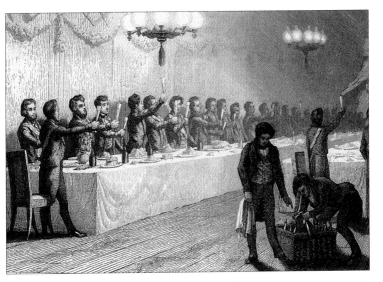

Preparing for toast and fire
French print c1790

in my best Turkish. Content that all had been clearly explained, I sat back to watch the proceedings. When the Ambassador's turn came, he executed the whole process to perfection. To my dismay, however, as the Cup was passed from one guest to the next, the Ambassador walked along, following the Cup. As discreetly as I could, I went up to him and politely said, "Ambassador, you are meant to sit down after drinking." He replied, "I cannot sit down . . . my teeth have fallen into the Cup.

I can emphasise that there is no obligation to drink from the cup and a bow of the head without drinking will suffice and no offence be given.

You are now ready for your after-dinner speech.

---

33 Quirky Facts
Quirky facts on the authenticity of which you can rely and which will surprise most listeners:

In the 1400s a law was enacted that a man was not allowed to beat his wife with a stick thicker than his thumb: hence the 'rule of thumb'.

It has been said that many years ago in Scotland a new game was invented. The rules stated: 'Gentlemen Only, Ladies Forbidden'. Thus the word 'GOLF' entered the English language.

Every day, more money is printed for the game of Monopoly than by the United States Treasury.

Men can read smaller print than women, but women can hear better.

It is impossible to lick your elbow.

Intelligent people have more traces of zinc and copper in their hair.

Bullet-proof vests, laser printers, fire escapes and windscreen wipers were all invented by women.

Multiply 111,111,111 by 111,111,111 and you will get 12,345,678,987,654,321.

34 Bonjour Monsieur

On the third day of our Mediterranean cruise with Anwar Dasat and our respective families, Anwar approached me and said, "There is a crazy Frenchman at my breakfast table and every morning when I join him he introduces himself." "What's his name?" I asked. "I know it by heart," said Anwar. "It is Bonjour Monsieur." I warned him that 'Bonjour Monsieur' is not a name but is French for 'Good Morning'. Clearly embarrassed by his lack of French knowledge, Anwar arrived early at the breakfast table the next morning. Before the Frenchmen had the opportunity to utter a word, Anwar said, "Bonjour Monsieur," to which the French gentleman replied, "Anwar Dasat," with a courteous bow.

35 Falklands Heroes

A few months after the successful Falklands campaign, Margaret Thatcher, then Prime Minister, was being driven back to 10 Downing Street when she noticed a beggar in the street. She stopped the car to challenge the man who, she felt, was a disgrace to society. On approaching him she read the notice on a little placard that hung from the beggar's neck: it read 'Falklands Campaign Veteran'. Well, this was different – the man was a hero and certainly not to be chastised. In a gesture of goodwill, Mrs Thatcher opened her purse and handed the man a crisp £50 note. He looked up at her in gratitude and said, "Muchas gracias, Señora."

36 Swiss Account

Corruption is a relative term, often depending on the culture of the country concerned. In the 1970s a new government decree in Peru required all Peruvian citizens to convert their foreign asset holdings into Peruvian currency. Not to do so was punishable by imprisonment. A government minister was dispatched to Switzerland to meet with the various Swiss bank presidents to identify Peruvian citizens with numbered Swiss accounts. At his first meeting with the president of the UBS, the minister explained about the new law passed in Peru requesting details and was quite naturally refused. He insisted: "I am here officially on behalf of the Peruvian government. Not complying with my request will endanger diplomatic relations between our countries." He threatened to no avail. "Mr President," the minister said in a conciliatory tone, "you will appreciate my situation. I have to return to my government with something in hand. I beg you to give me just one or two names, to save my face and job." "Out of the question," the bank's president replied. In exasperation the Peruvian minister took a gun out of his pocket and pointed it at the president. "Please understand," he said. "I am in a desperate situation." "Nothing will help you," persisted the adamant president. "You can shoot me but you will not obtain a single name from me." "In that case," said the minister, putting his gun away, "will you please open an account in my name?"

37 Windscreen Wipers

When the newest Mercedes M-Klasse 'Popemobil' model was ready for delivery, the Pope, fascinated by modern gadgets and facilities justifying the high expense to the Vatican, insisted on collecting it himself from the factory. As the car smoothly sped away under his control, it began to rain and, to the Pope's great consternation, the windscreen wipers did not work. He turned the car round and drove back to the factory, challenging the first engineer he came across. "How is this possible, in this super modern car costing an absolute fortune, that the windscreen wipers should not work?" he complained rather vexed. "But sir," said the Mercedes employee, "this is a unique Popemobil. It has a special button for when it rains. Do try it." He pointed to the left of the driving wheel. The Pope pressed the red knob . . . and the rain stopped.

38 Ming Jug for Cat

As a standard procedure I will enter any antique shop I pass. The smaller quaint village shops are particularly attractive and will sometimes yield a gem of an item at an acceptable price. On a gentle hillside, in a sleepy village in the Cotswolds, I had to duck my head to enter a tiny antiques shop. I immediately noticed a cat drinking milk from an original Ming dynasty china bowl in absolutely pristine condition. I hung around for a while and making my way to the door I said, "Such a lovely shop. I am sorry that there is nothing of particular interest . . . except for your cat. Is your cat for sale?" I enquired innocently. "It is," replied the shop owner. "It will cost you £50." That was a steep price for a cat but worth it for my devious plans. I paid the £50, took the cat under my arm, and as I was about to exit I said, "By the way, since I have the cat, what about the piece of china it was drinking from? Can I buy that too, please?" "I am very sorry, sir," replied the shop owner. "That Ming bowl is not for sale. We use it to sell cats."

39 Pay through Our Noses

An invoice I received from my son's school for the term fees had an accompanying letter, clearly not checked for spelling errors, stating '. . . we very much regret to announce an increase in the anal fees for the forthcoming year details of which will be forwarded in due course'. I decided to respond in the same vein, and never received an answer to my letter, which read, 'Thank you for your notification of the increased charges for the coming year. Could we, however, please continue to pay through our noses, as we have done to date?'

Chapter 2 summary

- Observe your audience
- Be among the first to arrive
- Listen rather than talk
- Do not get bogged down in conversation
- See that your lapel badge is prominent
- Avoid alcohol before you speak
- Eat sensibly
- Do not drink coffee
- Read the day's news
- Be modest and be brief
- Familiarise yourself with procedures (Masonic fire and loving cup)

Chapter 2 anecdotes

20 *Irrepressible Urge to Gossip*
21 *Buuur... geeeer... Kiiiiing*
22 *Welsh Rugby*
23 *Mr Horror*
24 *Separate Whiskies*
25 *Churchill: Whisky or Water First*
26 *Drunk After One Drink*
27 *High Street Off-Licence*
28 *American Embassy*
29 *Likey Speechey?*
30 *Pa, Ta – Amen*
31 *Bishop's Grace*
32 *Turkish Ambassador*

Chapter 2 additional anecdotes

33 *Quirky Facts*
34 *Bonjour Monsieur*
35 *Falklands Heroes*
36 *Swiss Account*
37 *Windscreen Wipers*
38 *Ming Jug for Cat*
39 *Pay Through Our Noses*

Soup Dish:
After-dinner speaking

1738 and all that

By 1738, on the 21st anniversary of the formation of Grand Lodge, Freemasons were in trouble. It wasn't that we were causing any problems or were in any way antisocial. The fact was that we had become far too fashionable. Ironically those self-same factors that had secured the success of Freemasonry soon after its inception, namely the recruitment of nobility, aristocracy and even royalty into our midst, were causing difficulties and distress. In one word, it was 'neglect'. Freemasonry was simply not important enough a cause to keep the ongoing interest of the upper classes, whose presence now dominated the echelons of the Society. Their neglect was about to cause the demise of the organisation. It was time for a new boost, and on 24 February 1735, Grand Lodge approved additions, alterations and revisions to be incorporated into a *New Book of Constitutions* which was published by James Anderson on 25 January 1738. This second edition of our *Constitutions* gives us, as mentioned in the previous chapter, the first detailed record of the historic events in 1717, and the relevant text on page 109 is worth quoting:

> 'Accordingly on St John Baptist's Day, in the 3rd year of King George I AD 1717 the Assembly and Feast of the Free and accepted Masons was held at the foresaid Goose and Gridiron Alehouse. Before dinner, the oldest Master Mason (now the Master of a lodge) in the Chair, proposed a List of proper candidates and the brethren by a majority of hands elected Mr Anthony Sayer, Gentleman, Grand Master of Masons, who being forthwith invested with the badges of Office and Power by the said oldest Master, and installed, was duly congratulated by the assembly who paid him the Homage.'

Two years later, at the Assembly and Feast on 24 June 1719, John Theophilus Desaguliers LLD and FR is duly 'invested, installed, congratulated and homaged' as the third Grand Master and 'he forthwith revived the old regular and peculiar Toasts or Healths of the Free Masons' and so it continues. Every Assembly has a feast attached to it and all pronouncements are made before or after dinner. And since 1719 we have enjoyed those 'peculiar Toasts or Healths' that are prevalent today. We are indeed a society with ancient and continuous traditions.

Opening Words

The cheese board has made its rounds and the coffee has been poured.

✠ **40**
How would you like your coffee, sir?" asks the waiter. "I like my coffee the way I like my women: strong, sweet and hot," is the reply. "Black or white, sir?" the waiter retorts.

The doors – when at a Masonic function – have been tyled and the usual wine takings and toasts have been dispensed with. Your turn is next. Sit upright, take several deep breaths, adjust your tie, check your flies (not a joke), straighten your waistcoat and jacket and make sure the napkin is not caught on your clothing, and when called upon, stand up slowly and deliberately. You should be feeling some nervousness, no matter how experienced you are. It will not improve matters if your host makes an inappropriate comment.

✠ **41**
"Are you ready for your speech, Mr Beresiner," asked my host on one occasion, "or shall we let them enjoy themselves a little longer?"

The flow of adrenalin in your bloodstream can only be of benefit. Place your chair in front of you so that you have a podium-like resting spot. Slowly count to three before you start speaking. Do not speak until there is absolute silence – this will raise a sense of anticipation and your next few words will determine the tone for the rest of your speech. If you can detect the sense of anticipation I refer to, and the more experienced you become the easier it will be for you to detect and capitalise on it to the maximum; for instance, by forgoing the standard and expected initial address. Instead of starting with "Mr President, ladies and gentlemen," commence with this subtle play on words: "I have something to say before I start speaking." After this introduction, proceed with a brief anecdote that sounds as if it is serious from the outset.

✠ **42**
"I have lost my pen. If anybody comes across it I would really appreciate its return. It is a small silver pen, not particularly valuable except for the sentiment attached to it. It belonged to my granddad. On his deathbed, with his very last breath . . . he sold it to me."

A serious face, timing and pauses are of paramount importance for the anecdote to have its maximum effect. I told this story as my opening remarks a dozen times on my ANZMRC tour of Australia and New Zealand in 2000. Each venue had a new and fresh audience and the story was always well received. On my return to England I had four pens sent to me by sympathetic members of my audience. There are only a number of stories where a serious face is essential for the anecdote to work, otherwise your smile and even a modest chuckle – joining the audience in their laughter at the end of the story – is perfectly acceptable and natural. There is nothing more important in telling an anecdote than timing. The silence between words and sentences, especially before the punch line, are the absolute determining factor in making a good story excellent. You will be able to judge the responsiveness of your audience by their reaction. Do not forget at the end of the deviation from the expected protocol, to now revert to the standard greeting as if you were about to start your speech. Face your host, address him and the dignitaries in the approved manner, express your appreciation at being invited and continue as originally intended.

Opening Address

The opening address to the dignitaries, whether Masonic or otherwise, should be brief and succinct but do not forget protocol. In an exclusively Masonic environment your own Masonic rank will dictate your opening address. This is discussed in greater detail in the next chapter. In the 'civilian' world, the protocol for forms of address is dictated by extensive rules and regulations to be found in different sources. One error that keeps being repeated at festive boards applies to the Loyal Toast, which should simply be 'The Queen'. It is only when the Queen is personally present that the toast would correctly state 'Her Majesty the Queen'. Our own Grand Master, HRH The Duke of Kent, is of royal blood, and his brother, HRH Prince Michael of Kent, is Grand Master of the Mark Master Masons of England. At times, both grace us with their presence at our meetings and festivities. Whenever in a Masonic environment they are to be referred to as 'The Most Worshipful Grand Master'. The correct form of address in any other circumstance is 'His Royal Highness', which applies to all members of a royal family. As an aside, the reason that Prince Michael has the title of prince whilst his older brother's title is duke is because in the British royal family, a son of a monarch is a royal prince and he is given the title of duke on his marriage. The princes' father, Prince George, was made Duke of Kent when he married Princess Marina of Greece. The title Duke of Kent was therefore inherited by Prince Michael's older brother, as it is only the eldest son that inherits the ducal title: the remaining siblings remain princes.

In June 2003 the Crown Office prepared a detailed listing for Forms of Address, both oral and in writing. Titles of nobility or peerages are granted by the Monarch and the prefixes for the five ranks in the Peerage, in order of seniority, will be familiar to Freemasons because they correspond to those in our own hierarchy. Thus, the Most Noble refers to Dukes, The Most Honourable to Marquesses, The Right Honourable to Earls, Viscounts and Barons and The Honourable to the younger sons of Earls and all children of

Viscounts and Barons. The corresponding ladies' titles are Duchess, Marchioness, Countess, Viscountess and Baroness. Our own Pro Grand Master is a peer, and when present at Masonic functions he should simply be addressed as 'Most Worshipful Pro Grand Master', without any further appellations. The Crown Office listing explains, for instance, that all Privy Counsellors should be correctly addressed by their official titles, when applicable, prefixed by 'The Right Honourable' and not by their personal names. Cabinet ministers, it should be remembered, are made Privy Counsellors as a result of their taking office.

The same applies to English judges, the Lord Chancellor and the five Heads of Divisions who are all Privy Counsellors. The Lord Mayor of the City of London will always be referred to as 'My Lord Mayor' and the appellation 'Sir' before a name indicates that the holder is a baronet or knight of some order of chivalry. In every case they are entitled to the prefix 'Sir', followed by the forename. Always use the forename by which the holder wishes to be known. In the case of women, the prefix becomes Dame. The complexity and detailed directives have, I trust, been amply illustrated and the advice I strongly recommend is consultation *before* your speech. Obtain details from the Director of Ceremonies or the Toast Master as to who the guests present will be and find out the exact and correct modes of address. It will not only be embarrassing for you but also discourteous to the guest concerned for you to get the opening address wrong. It would be an uncomfortable start to a speech.

Do not Gesticulate

It is apparently impossible to speak without some motion of your arms and hands. Different nationalities react in different ways. It is a matter of nature and habit. Controlled gestures are, however, an excellent tool for use in speeches when wanting to emphasise a point or underline a word or, most effectively, to illustrate a funny story.

43
Two jet pilots in a dogfight over the Mediterranean shot each other down simultaneously and both bailed out of their respective fighter planes. One parachute opened, and on his descent, the pilot could see that the second pilot's chute had failed. As the doomed pilot was about to hurtle past him, the first pilot grabbed hold of him in a strong hug. "A few seconds ago we tried to kill each other," said the grateful survivor, "and now you save my life! Why?" he asked. "I don't know," replied the first, spreading his arms wide.

This story will be difficult to visualise in its written version but act it out whilst speaking and you can be assured of a hearty response. You may choose to insert sworn enemies as the two adversaries: Germans and Englishmen in the Second World War or Israelis and Arabs for today. Your gestures will only work for you when you are totally in control of them. Unnecessary gesturing only detracts from your speech. Irrelevant gestures attract attention away from your words. The general rule is that you do not use your arms and hands except consciously, to make specific points. The best place to rest your hands is on the chair placed in front of you as suggested above. Do not keep your hands in your pockets as that is considered to be ill mannered. Different gestures have different meanings. Never clench your fist as it is considered aggressive and threatening. Do not point or wag an index finger; it is seen as derogatory to your audience as if speaking down to them.

Length of Speech

Towards the end of your speech, the audience should always feel that they could have happily listened to more on what you had to say. Do not be persuaded by your host to speak for longer than you feel it appropriate. An after-dinner speech, unless intended as a combined lecture and speech, should last between five and ten minutes at the very most. Prepare your speech so that you allow yourself enough flexibility to cut it shorter or continue a little longer. In the speech, having two or more 'endings' will allow you to select one or the other at will. As you speak, and as you gain experience, it will be easy to judge how your speech is being received. The response of your audience may be influenced by various factors, not necessarily just your words. For instance, if time is running short and the evening has been drawn out, as the last speaker, you should be considerate and be very brief, with one amusing tale and an appropriate ending. If your speech is followed by formal entertainment or dancing, remain conscious of the anticipation being experienced by your audience and keep your speech appropriately brief. The time to allow yourself the full ten to twenty minutes is when you are the guest speaker, the main event of the evening, and having started your speech, you can sense your audience responding and warming to you.

44
You will not wish to find yourself in the shoes of the speaker who finished his lecture somehow and limped off amidst roars of silence from the audience.

Do Not Self-Deprecate

Be very careful with self-deprecating stories that should always be avoided unless they are very subtle and delicate. They may backfire. Never apologise. In both instances a lack of confidence in yourself will become apparent. Sentences such as, 'I rise from the ranks of the lowly with humility' or 'I consider myself the least worthy,' should be avoided at all costs – they are meaningless and insincere.

45
I was very proud to be invited to lecture at an asylum for the mentally handicapped. The nurse in charge approached me before my brief lecture and asked that I should ignore any interruptions or interference by my audience on whose behalf he apologised in advance. Within moments of starting my speech, one of the patients in the second row shouted "Rubbish!" I ignored him, as advised and continued to speak. A few minutes later the same man shouted out, "Absolute nonsense. Sit down!" I carried on undeterred and was interrupted for the rest of my talk with constant abuse: "Garbage," "Baloney," "Twaddle," "Enough already," and some less polite expletives, all by the one man. I ended my talk to applause and the nurse thanked me profusely, apologising again for the interruption and commenting: "One piece of good news you may appreciate, Mr Beresiner. Those are the first sensible words our patient Mr Smith has spoken in two years."

Be Yourself and Natural

The best after-dinner speakers are natural speakers. The word 'natural' has been grossly misinterpreted. By natural, I mean that you are able to *appear* to be natural. There is no such thing as a natural born speaker. Every successful speaker has worked very hard and practised a great deal to appear to be a natural speaker. To be natural means speaking with ease and knowledge in a simple, understandable language, avoiding hyperbole and sophisticated vocabulary, not worrying about the odd mispronunciation or hesitation. It is essential that you do not make any guttural sounds whilst pausing to think or starting a new sentence. The 'Ehhhhh' sound, so often heard when a speaker stops to take breath or to think before a new sentence, is very disruptive and surprisingly common, especially amongst experienced speakers such as politicians. 'Natural' also means that you speak from your heart and mean what you say – do not pretend. Be yourself and bear in mind that you are not on stage as an actor or a comedian would be. You are a guest selected from your equals to speak to them. Make sure you are not patronising. All audiences will prefer a simple self-explanatory story. Do not try to be clever and test your audience's intelligence. On the other hand, be sure not to insult them by underestimating their intelligence. See how fast they respond when you use a subtler anecdote. I already have suggested that you start with, "There is something I would like to say before I start speaking."

46
Another similar testing story is the anecdote of a patient who is informed by his doctor that there is both good and bad news about his health. "The good news," says the doctor, "is that you are definitely not a hypochondriac."

The speed of the response to this anecdote can be a good guide to the quality of the response you will have for the rest of your speech. All these aspects of speechmaking entail a delicate balance, which will become apparent as you become a more experienced speaker. Remember that you are standing up to entertain and not to impress. Use all the talents available to you and avoid those that you only *think* may succeed. If you are fortunate to have an aptitude to mimic, do not hesitate to use your gift as long as you are genuinely good at it. If your ability to impersonate applies only to one well-known character, write your speech so that you can bring the person concerned into your performance and use your mimicking ability to the utmost. Be sure that the character is definitely well known to everyone in the audience. To select a local politician or a minor television character will not do. If in doubt, do not do it.

Do Not Be Put Off

Confidence consists of not being put off by anything. There are several factors that could disrupt your plans, thoughts and your speech. Ignore them all and remain confident in what you have prepared and what you have to say. There may be speakers before you, who introduce you and do so with particular panache and expertise. If you know a speaker to be a lawyer or barrister you can be assured that he will be a good speaker.

47

When I left law school I was warned that I was entering an unpopular profession. I realised just how true this was some 20 years later when my daughter Anad, a primary school teacher, told me that she had been asking the boys and girls in her class what their respective fathers did professionally. One replied that his dad was a musician, another was a bank manager and the father of a third little girl was an engineer. "How about your dad, Matthew?" asked my daughter. "What does he do?" She did not expect the reply she was given. "My dad," replied Matthew somewhat defiantly, "plays the piano in a brothel!" Quite disconcerted, Anad called young Matthew's father at the next opportunity and warned him, "Your son has been saying that you are a musician in a house of ill repute." "I am very sorry," apologised Mr Matthew senior. "I am afraid my son is embarrassed by the fact that I am a lawyer."

Never refer to the brilliance of a previous speaker with statements such as "How does one follow that?" or worse still, "I cannot pretend to emulate the previous speaker." Please do not ever say, "On a more serious note . . ." It sounds as if you are telling the audience that they should have been laughing at your previous comments. These are absolute no-nos. Consider yourself fortunate in comparison to Victorian times when in between speeches, songs and ballads were sung, such as the trendy Gilbert and Sullivan operas, which became popular at the start of the 20th century. That would have been competition. Never compare yourself or try to compete with a previous speaker. Remember that you are *different,* not necessarily better and certainly not worse, simply different. Remain confident and trust yourself. Do not change anything in your speech because of what a speaker before you may have said. If you had planned to refer to the previous speaker, do so without changing any of your original words. There are obvious exceptions to these comments: if you feel you can capitalise on what has been said, do so, especially if you can use it with humour. For instance, when you are introduced at some length, your opening words can be: "Thank you for those kind words, though I fear my speech may not be quite as long as the introduction." Be careful not to appear arrogant when you say as an alternative, "Thank you for that generous introduction. I could not have written it better myself."

Hecklers

On rare occasions you may be interrupted by a comment from a member of the audience. You have one of two options: ignore it completely and continue with your speech or stop and meet head on whatever challenge has been thrown at you. In the latter case, if you cannot think of an extremely suitable short retort, do not try a clever quip. It may well bounce back at you. It will be better for you to ask the interrupter to repeat himself and tackle whatever his subject is. If you feel confident that he will *not* take you up on your offer, invite him to join you at the podium or top table. At times it is not the words but the status of the speaker before you that may be disconcerting. You do not necessarily need to respond to a comment from the audience. An interruption is an entirely different matter from a question. You can thank the person concerned politely and continue with your speech. Be very careful as the time taken in any such incident is at your own expense and your time is valuable.

Ending your Speech

I will not withhold from stating the obvious and much repeated statement that every speech has to have a beginning (anecdotal), a body (the serious stuff) and an ending (ideally, memorable).

48
My granddaughter Issad, when only eight years old, got it right when she asked me, "Saba (that is what she calls me), do you know why an elephant has a tail?" "No, darling, tell me why does an elephant have a tail?" "So that it doesn't end suddenly."

The ending of your speech needs to be brief and, if possible, encompass the subject matter, so long as there was one. If your after-dinner speech has consisted essentially of several anecdotes, it is fairly easy to conclude it with an appropriate story, thus ending with one more anecdote, before saying thank you and sitting down, which will suffice. If you had a clear-cut theme, as I recommend you should always have, then a suitable anecdote

The Best of Manners at the Dining Table
After Gilray c1790 (Guildhall)

on that theme will be most appropriate. Often opening and closing stories are interchangeable. You can end with a story that would have been suitable as an opener. It is the context in which you place it that will make it suitable.

49
I was the guest speaker at a Rotary Club Anniversary and was carried away by some of the emotion and excitement of the evening's proceedings and suddenly realised that I had exceeded by far the time allocated to me. "I am very sorry, ladies and gentlemen," I said quite truthfully. "I left my watch at home and have exceeded my time." To which a gentleman in the front replied, "Don't worry about it. There is a calendar just behind you."

Writing your Speech Down

Always write your after-dinner speech out in full, no matter how short or long. As a secondary process, shorten it in stages until you have single lines or even single words as memory triggers. The more experienced you become and the better you know your subject, the fewer notes you will need. Ensure that you are familiar with the format of your notes and can easily refer to points of consequence. Use colour pens to emphasise different aspects and sections of your speech: for instance, to differentiate between anecdotes and serious comments. Always have an additional summarised page of dates and names with you. Remember to verify the pronunciation of names before speech-time. Never contemplate reading out your speech in full. You should only be seen to be looking at your notes to refresh your memory, not to read full sentences. If you get in the habit of not using notes from the start, it will become easier and easier as you gain more experience.

You should, early on, be able to reach a stage where it is only the sequence of the words that need sorting on a small sheet of paper to enable you to deliver a full speech word perfect. Consider that your audience does not know what you are about to tell them and, more importantly, they certainly do not know what you have *not* told them. Once you realise this you will feel much less concerned when you forget to mention a fact or event. You should never retract or use the words "I forgot to tell you," "I should have said," or express any similar sentiments. Just carry on speaking and you will often find that not mentioning a story or anecdote actually improves your speech. Having reduced your extended speech to a series of single words that fit on the back of an ordinary visiting card, always take the full version with you for rehearsal purposes. Whilst you may be rehearsing your speech using the memory triggers you prepared, it is not a bad idea to have a glance and read through it all once or twice during the course of the evening when the opportunity presents itself.

Links

The greatest pitfall when preparing your speech without writing it out in full is the lack of links. In your mind, you may be confident that moving from one subject to the next with a suitable anecdote in between will be easy to deliver, so long as you remember the headings for the three paragraphs. You are wrong. You need to link them together so that the transition from a serious subject into an anecdote has relevance. It applies to an equal extent when you continue after the anecdote. You will need another link to return to your theme. These links do not come naturally. You have to create them often by manipulating words and sentences that lead into the next subject. A lack of links is disruptive for an after-dinner speaker, whereas it is perfectly natural for a stand-up comedian. The latter is just telling one story after another and his only concern is to get a laugh after each joke. This is not true of an after-dinner speaker whose speech has to have a story and flow naturally even when interspersed with anecdotes. Links allow that smooth flow and prevent awkward silences or an unrelated and apparent sudden change of subject.

Pronunciation

Everyone has an accent. It may be one that is comfortable to the ear or one of an easily recognisable origin. Occasionally it is totally unidentifiable.

The point to remember is that the harshness or gentleness of your accent lies in the listener's ear. So, unless you are blessed or trained, you need to learn to speak slowly and deliberately. Do not be misled by your knowledge of the English language, especially if you have a strong foreign accent – such knowledge does not imply that you can be understood clearly. Pronounce words fully and, most importantly, if you mention names be sure that you have both the spelling and pronunciation correct. You do not need to get professional assistance with phonetics to learn the correct pronunciation of a name. Invent your own system and be sure to remember it. This will apply equally whether you are referring to historical characters long dead, the president of the USA or a fellow host sitting next to you at dinner.

50
It was embarrassing to hear our third Grand Master, John Desaguliers, referred to as John Desagulies and rather amusing to have the president of Iran, at the time of writing, Mahmoud Ahmadinejad, referred to openly and without apology as "I'm-in-my-dinner-jacket."

You also need, when appropriate and beyond the opening addresses, to correctly identify the titles and ranks of those you refer to. It is all a matter of preparation, practice and rehearsal before you speak. Never underestimate the occasion or the audience you will be addressing – it may be a small group of brethren at a private party or a gala dinner at the Mansion House. Treat each occasion as important as the next and prepare accordingly. You will be treated with equal respect no matter what the occasion is and your hosts deserve the same treatment.

Repeating Anecdotes

The more successful you are, the more frequently you will be invited for a return visit and another speech. You will definitely need to change the theme of your address. Do not worry if you cannot recall the anecdotes already used on a previous occasion. Firstly, no matter how successful you were, the likelihood of your anecdotes being remembered by all present is extremely remote. Secondly, there is never an identical audience at any two meetings no matter how private the club. And finally, most importantly, a good story well told and in context is like a familiar piece of music. You can hear it again and again and you will always enjoy it. This does not mean that you should only have one set piece of text and anecdotes and keep repeating them on every occasion you are asked to speak. It is tempting to do so because you can improve your set speech every time you give it. Early on, alter the theme and implement new anecdotes even when not necessary. Practice makes perfect.

Professional Writers & Licence

You cannot plagiarise verbal statements and there is no reason whatsoever not to use somebody else's speech and jokes. You also have the option to employ a professional speechwriter. In either case that habit may spoil your own development as a speaker. Use a speechwriter, whether a professional or a qualified amateur, only where the subject matter is such that you yourself would have difficulties in researching the facts. For instance, should you have the opportunity to speak at a political event of some kind, the knowledge you will need about the political ambience may be such that someone directly involved would be better able to advise what may and may not be said. Such a situation may also occur if you have been invited to introduce another speaker at an academic conference.

51

I was never able to deliver the speech I prepared when I was invited to speak at the Annual Dinner of the National Association of Amnesiacs – I was the only one that turned up. Though I did, on one single occasion in my long speaking career, receive a standing ovation. I had been addressing the International Pain Prevention Society for Haemorrhoid Sufferers.

A speaker is allowed considerable licence with the accuracy of his statements. When writing, it is critical for your facts and dates to be accurate. That does not apply when speaking. You need not be too concerned if a fact is not exact or whether a date is absolutely precise. You certainly need not worry if you substitute a month or a year for another. If you are aware that you are unable to recall a fact or date do say, "If I am not mistaken" or "approximately" but do not apologise. Never pre-empt any part of your speech by stating that you are not sure of the accuracy of your facts and dates: it will detract from the flow of your speech. You are also allowed a great deal of licence when personalising anecdotes, whether speaking about yourself or a third party. The more realistic the story sounds the better it will be received, no matter how obviously untrue.

Adjustments

A ready-made speech will always be enhanced by last moment adjustments to incorporate statements of direct relevance to your audience. This can most readily and easily be achieved by a direct reference in your speech to the people you have been speaking with at dinner. A story that you may have ready in your speech can often be personalised by assigning it to a named individual, preferably already known to those in the room. It is always important, when using another person as the subject of your humour, not to cause any offence. Always use your humour with dignity and make a point of not telling jokes. An after-dinner speaker must be a storyteller, a raconteur with anecdotes, and not be a joker. The more information you have obtained – of the venue, the guests of honour, your audience and so forth – the more relevant references you can make and the better your speech will be appreciated.

Risqué Stories

In principle do not use risqué stories.

52
I was about to introduce the experienced guest of honour speaker, Miguel Pierce, who, to my surprise, looked decidedly nervous. In response to my prompting he finally explained that he was eager to get back home. He had attended his annual check-up and his doctor, who otherwise declared him to be in excellent health for a 66-year-old, asked him when was the last time that he had made love. Miguel was not embarrassed by the question; after all this was his doctor. He was embarrassed by the fact that he could not remember. On the insistence of the doctor he finally phoned his wife at home and said, "Darling, when was the last time we made love?" After a few moments' silence, his wife replied, "Who is that speaking?"

Repeating this story is as risqué a tale as you may be allowed to tell. In some circles even this may be considered a little over the top. If you are not absolutely certain that a story will be acceptable to every single person in the room, do not use it.

53
My 60th birthday was a traumatic event by any standards. I was out of bed early, showered and inspected my middle age spread with greater care than usual. I was looking okay, reasonably fit and reasonably content. When I arrived at the office, I knew my long-suffering secretary would not have forgotten my birthday and she welcomed me with a gentle kiss on my cheek. "Tell me the truth," I asked, taking a stance in profile. "I do not really look 60, do I?" "No, you don't," she replied without a smile. "But you used to."

Sex

There are three risqué areas you have to take into account: sex, religion and politics. Each of these areas can be totally avoided or effectively used in anecdotes that are mild, carefully selected and give no offence. The judgement as to whether they may be offensive or not has to be left to the audience. What you may consider acceptable and funny may well be offensive and not at all amusing to other people. You, as a speaker, have to judge your audience, not your risqué stories. If in doubt do not tell the story.

54
Two Frenchmen, two Italians, two Englishmen and two Grand Officers of the United Grand Lodge of England, together with four young ladies, were

shipwrecked and marooned on a desert island. Each one of the ladies joined their male colleagues. The French came to a speedy agreement and their female companion agreed to spend time with one of them on Mondays, Wednesdays and Fridays, and with the other one on the remaining days of the week, resting on the Sunday. The two aggressive Italians had it out in a duel: one killed the other and had the girl to himself. The Englishmen did not hesitate: they killed the girl and enjoyed each other's company for the rest of time. As to the Grand Officers . . . they still await instructions from Grand Lodge.

Do not repeat this story in the presence of a Grand Officer unless you are one yourself. Whilst avoiding sexually orientated stories, unless very mild and reliably amusing and inoffensive, be particularly attentive not to be sexist. It makes no difference whether there are ladies in the audience or not. If in doubt do not tell it.

Religion & Creed

Our sensitivities apply to all discrimination and here lies the key in telling religious or ethnic stories. If we accept that there is just one God up there and each one of us has a different way of seeing him, then interdenominational stories, as long as they are not offensive, are okay.

55
There is a special spirit of community unity in Golders Green manifest in the Church of England's proximity to the local Bank Leumi Le-Israel. The former has a large banner in its grounds declaring 'Jesus Saves'. Some wit has spread graffiti on the bank's wall reading in response: 'Moses Invests'.

56
My son Yug's first visit to Harrods department store in Knightsbridge was late in December on his eighth birthday. As soon as we entered the decorated store, Yug was picked off his feet by a Father Christmas in full dress, who placed him on his knee and asked: "What is your name, little boy?" "I am Yug," replied my son coyly. "And what would you like for Christmas, Yug?" asked Father Christmas, first obtaining my nod of approval. "We do not celebrate Christmas," said Yug. "We are Jewish and we celebrate Chanukah," he explained. "That's okay," said Father Christmas. "What would you like for Chanukah?" Yug thought for just a moment and said, "Can I have a Christmas tree, please?"

Do not venture into the field of religious stories unless your whole theme is religious or nationalistic and you are speaking at a level of self-awareness acceptable and comfortable to your audience. There are plenty of other stories to be told. If in doubt, avoid it. I will admit that I heard some of the most amusing Jewish stories from gentile colleagues told to me in private and not in a speech they were making.

*Gran'pop goes
through the chair*
Lawson Wood Postcard
1920s

57
Two ladies speak to each other whilst shopping. One says: "I am a little concerned with my eight year old. He plays with his genitals all the time." "Don't worry, darling," replies the other. "Some of my best friends are genitals."

Much of what has been said about religion applies to ethnic stories. It is an interesting question, for instance, whether stories about Jews are religious or ethnic. A similar question arises with Irish Catholics and Protestants, as well as blacks, Chinese and Japanese. In most instances religion naturally extends to ethnicity and ethnic tales are best told by a member of the same ethnic group. Avoid Jewish stories unless you are of the faith or Irish stories unless you are Irish and so forth. You have to be a very good judge of taste if you want to break the rule.

58
At the peak of the Irish troubles a terrorist pointed his gun at a terrified individual in a deserted street. "Are you Catholic or Protestant?" enquired the terrorist threateningly. "I am Jewish," replied the petrified victim. "I must be the luckiest Arab in the whole of Ireland," was the retort.

The Last Degree
USA Are you a
Mason? postcard
series 1920s

Politics

There is a major difference between politically risqué stories and sexual or religious ones. With politics the greater danger is that you will raise controversy rather than offend anyone. Politics is a sensitive subject only because so many people have such widely differing political views and so many take their political views very seriously indeed. Consider the disagreement and antagonism that you may cause by raising politically sensitive subjects, whether they are of local council consequence or international disputes between two nations. It is always the context within which your statements are made that will allow them to be perfectly acceptable or cause problems. It is not for nothing that we do not discuss politics or religion in Freemasonry. Your whole theme may be political and anecdotes relevant to what you have to say, as examples or pinpointing facts, will be acceptable.

59
Winston Churchill and his legendary political adversary, Lady Astor, have a range of quotable exchanges: "You are ugly, Lady Astor," Churchill is reputed to have said at some reception or other. "You are drunk, Winston," replied Lady Astor. "Yes, I am," Churchill replied. "But tomorrow, I will be sober."

Another classical exchange was Lady Astor's frustrations with Churchill, which culminated in her saying, "If you were my husband, Winston, I would poison your coffee." To which Churchill replied, "If I was your husband, Lady Astor, I would drink it."

On the other hand, to attack a political party, the prime minister or adversely comment on the Chairman or members of a local council out of context for the mere sake of creating amusement, will not be well received.

Let us next look at purely Masonic circumstances.

Chapter 3 summary
- Sit upright, take a deep breath etc
- Do not speak until there is absolute silence
- Enunciate your words clearly and loudly
- Do not gesticulate
- Do not self-deprecate
- Never apologise
- Avoid hyperbole and sophisticated words
- Do not make any guttural sounds whilst pausing
- Entertain – do not impress
- Do not be put off your speech – you are different
- Get spelling and pronunciation correct
- Personalise anecdotes
- You are not a stand-up comedian
- Use humour with dignity
- An after-dinner speaker is a storyteller
- Do not use risqué stories
- Judge your audience, not your stories
- Do not be sexist
- If in doubt do not use it

Chapter 3 anecdotes

Knife and Fork Mason & Liveryman
Gentlemen's Magazine 1772 (Guildhall)

Fish Dish:
Formal Masonic toasts and speeches

1751 and all that

English Freemasonry reached a major crossroads when, on 17 July 1751, five lodges whose membership consisted exclusively of Irish Freemasons met as a General Assembly at the Turks Head tavern in Greek Street, London, and founded the Grand Lodge of England According to the Old Institutions. This became known as the 'Antients Grand Lodge', and the earlier Premier Grand Lodge of 1717 was dubbed as the 'Moderns Grand Lodge', terms that have remained in use to this day. The Antients were formed as a rival body to the existing Grand Lodge and their strong Irish origins and influence led them on a course of divergence of ritual and practice, which was distinctly different and quite innovative in comparison with the traditional practices of the Moderns. There was no deviation, however, from the subject of eating, drinking and the festive boards. In the various editions of *Ahiman Rezon,* the Constitutions of the Antients first published in 1756, Laurence Dermott, the dynamic and dedicated secretary of the Antients, accused the Moderns effectively of being flippant. He stated, for instance, that the letters J and B on the pillars drawn by the Tyler referred to Jamaica and Barbados rum 'to distinguish where these liquors are to be placed in lodge'. He called the ritual of the Moderns the 'Knife and Fork Degree' because of their emphasis on the festive board, around which the ceremonies took place. The term 'Knife and Fork Mason' is still in use today.

> *I do not attend the meetings*
> *for I've not the time to spare.*
> *But every time they have a feast*
> *you will surely find me there.*
> *I cannot help with the degrees*
> *for I do not know the work.*
> *But I can applaud the speakers,*
> *and handle a knife and fork.*
> *I'm so rusty in the ritual,*
> *it seems like Greek to me.*
> *But practice has made me perfect*
> *in the Knife and Fork Degree.'*

Bro Richard L. Kurtz

One of the more interesting references to food is to be found in the handwritten records by Dermott on 4 March 1752. Dermott claimed that a number of named brethren made formal complaints against Thomas Phealon and John Macky, better known as the 'Leg of Mutton Masons', who appear to 'have initiated many persons for the mean consideration of a leg of mutton for dinner or supper, to the disgrace of the Ancient Craft'. The said brethren were dismissed from Grand Lodge.

Formal Speeches

Formal Masonic speechmaking is limited to two areas alone: in lodge and at the festive board. The protocol that is followed in lodge is such that you, like every other member, will have become familiar with the repetitious procedure over the years. By the time you have the opportunity to stand in lodge to speak, you will have learned the form just by having seen and listened to your seniors since your initiation. Nonetheless there are a number of minor comments worth making.

60
When the secretary of my lodge sadly passed to the Grand Lodge above, an over-enthusiastic Bro Horace, in his quest to become the lodge secretary, approached the Worshipful Master without due protocol. "WM," he asked. "I know it is only a few hours since our Bro secretary's demise, but do you think there is any chance for me to replace him?" The Master thought for a few minutes and replied, "I have no objection at all. I will have a word with the undertakers and see if it can be arranged with them."

Speaking in Lodge

Outside of ritual work, when different regulations apply, when you stand to speak in lodge, the general rule is that you salute the Worshipful Master irrespective of your rank and no matter who you are addressing in lodge. The Worshipful Master may acknowledge your salute with a bow of the head but does not salute in return, nor does he salute when addressing any member of the lodge. Having saluted the Worshipful Master, lower the sign before continuing and salute once more when finished, before sitting. A speaker with his sign up whilst speaking looks awkward and uncomfortable, especially a Secretary or Treasurer, who use notes and refer to paperwork on the desk. Reports given to the brethren should be clearly addressed to the brethren. Whatever your function or office in lodge, when you make a report, look around at the individual brethren sitting in lodge, and position yourself so that you can be seen by every brother. Move from your seat, if need be, to a more prominent position. Speak clearly and loudly so that you are audible to all and project your voice to the furthest corner in the temple. If you are using notes, look at them but only speak after you raise your head, unless, of course, you are reading your notes in which case hold them at a height that is convenient to view. Be brief with your reports. Make them factual and simple so that they are understood by all and be brief. Brevity not only ensures that your report is heard but that it is also absorbed and remembered by the brethren.

At the Festive Board

At the festive board the story is different. Here we have speeches that are intended to be more light-hearted and entertaining, though brevity still applies.

61
George Bernard Shaw may have exceeded the required briefness when invited to address an academic audience on the subject of wine, women and song. He stood to great applause and said, "Ladies and gentlemen, it gives me the greatest pleasure . . ." and then sat down without saying a further word.

There are many different circumstances under which you may have the opportunity to speak at the festive board.

62
The late and lamented Bro Cyril Batham, a well-known historian and dedicated Freemason, was the founding Master of a City lodge and determined to establish a new tradition for after-dinner speeches. At his installation meeting, following the festive board, he stood up unprompted after the meal, and said, "Brethren, I take it on myself to toast myself as Worshipful Master on this auspicious occasion. I respond with a hearty thank you. May I also use this opportunity to welcome all our many guests and invite a response on the understanding that if anybody should choose to do so, they will never be invited again." The brethren stood and drank and the tradition in the lodge is ongoing to this day.

63
Bro Cyril, a ladies' man by any standard throughout his life, reached the mature age of 80 with just two interests left in life: women and Freemasonry. He declared at one meeting that he felt he was getting far too old to pursue Freemasonry.

Wine Taking vs Toasting

Wine takings, as opposed to toasts, are standard and well established. It is important to remember that when taking wine, the brother or brethren mentioned in the wine taking stand up to drink from their glass; that means that the parties concerned all stand up. This includes every brother with whom wine is being taken, irrespective of rank. It may be the Provincial Grand Master honouring the lodge with his presence, or the newly initiated brother enjoying his first festive board. When taking wine you stand up. That is why, for instance, the Director of Ceremonies may state that the Master will take wine with all present and requests that they remain seated whilst he will stand. It is when a toast is given – as opposed to a wine taking – that the recipient of the toast remains seated, lifts his glass in acknowledgement but does *not* drink. It is worth emphasising that deviating from the normal standard and dignified wine takings is frowned upon and discouraged. Cross-toasting, where a brother shouts out the name or rank of another and both stand to drink, is unacceptable. It was embarrassing to witness this practice extend to the brethren concerned standing on their chairs and then on the table whilst cross-toasting.

Opening Address

As stated, it is your own rank that will determine your opening address. As a Past Master or Master Mason, you need to pay respect to your seniors and your opening address should be: 'Worshipful Master, Grand Officers and Brethren'. (Add Brother Wardens after Worshipful Master, in the Provinces.) Avoid the tedious and totally unnecessary practice of including every conceivable group in your listing. There is nothing more boring and unpromising than the following start to a speech: 'Worshipful Master, Grand Officers, Distinguished Brethren, Bro Senior and Bro Junior Wardens, Holders of London Grand Rank, Senior London Grand Rank, Metropolitan and Provincial Grand Lodges and Overseas Grand Lodges, Brother guests and visitors and Brethren of the lodge, good evening.'

An extended address should only be given in the presence of a Grand Officer whose prefix is Very, Right or Most Worshipful – thus only those above the rank of Assistant Grand Master should be mentioned in your opening address immediately following the Master. There may be present Grand Masters from other jurisdictions, who should be accorded the same courtesy as our own Grand Officers and addressed as Most Worshipful. As a Grand Officer yourself, there is no need for niceties and 'Worshipful Master' and 'Brethren' will suffice. There are naturally deviations in each instance, and in the Provinces for instance, it is customary to include Brother Wardens after Worshipful Master, in all opening addresses. When the Metropolitan or Provincial Grand Master is present, he should be singled out, irrespective of your own rank. These are generalisations and you need to use common sense on each occasion. It is impossible to cater in writing for every opportunity and event.

Responding as a Grand Officer

As a Grand Officer, whether a member of the lodge or not, you will normally be invited to respond, should you wish to do so, following the toast to the Pro Grand Master and Grand Officers. Do not accept the invitation unless you have something of consequence that you wish to convey. If you decide

The Third Degree Drink
USA Are You a Mason? postcard series 1920s

to speak, it will be sufficient for you to address the Worshipful Master and brethren and there is no need to acknowledge your fellow Grand Officers who may be present. It is not usual for a Grand Officer to be invited to respond to any other toasts given at the festive board, such as the toast to the guests. Exceptions occur, and if you are known or recognised as an entertaining speaker, you will find yourself called upon with ever increasing frequency. When you stand up, you do so as a representative of the whole army of Grand Officers present and past. Your words and demeanour need to reflect that fact and you should speak accordingly. Some who know you personally may remember what you say as your own statements. The majority, however, who may not know you, will only remember your speech as the one given by the Grand Officer who responded.

Be dignified and be brief. In the Provinces and Metropolitan London, convey the greetings of the PGM or the MGM, do mention any 'hot' Grand Lodge news item the brethren may be discussing amongst themselves, but only if you are *au fait* with the facts. Do not speculate and most certainly do not second-guess events about which you know nothing. Speak responsibly. A Grand Officer's apron and collar do not come with foresight and wisdom. Remain modest and you will remain popular. Avoid criticising the lodge in any manner whatsoever and never leave early, particularly as a Visiting Officer. Allow that privilege, or enjoy it, when you are part of the high executive. So far as protocol is concerned at table, and in lodge for that matter, you are entitled but not obligated to take your place in order of Grand Lodge seniority at the top table or the East in lodge, on the Master's right. There is nothing that stops you from sitting amongst the brethren in lodge, when, for instance, it is a crowded meeting or when a lower ranking brother is your guest or host. The same applies to the festive board and you may at anytime forgo the privilege of being on the top table and sit at one of the extension sprigs.

At an Installed Masters' Lodge

When invited to speak at an installed Masters' lodge, remain aware of the special standing of the brethren you are addressing: they are all Masters or Past Masters of their respective lodges. There will usually be a healthy sprinkling of Provincial or Metropolitan Grand Officers and often a generous presence of Grand Officers. They are all experienced Masons, as well as being a captive audience. They are there in the knowledge that they will be addressed by a guest speaker and are ready to listen. Avoid any basic comments you would normally direct to members of an ordinary lodge who may include young Masons, even below the rank of Master Mason. Here, at an installed Masters' lodge, you can safely presume that your audience are all knowledgeable and aware of the basic principles of Freemasonry.

Toast to the Worshipful Master

It is customary, though far from obligatory, for the toast to the Worshipful Master to be given by the Immediate Past Master. At the installation meeting this is almost invariably the case. During the remainder of the year the Master may well invite other brethren, usually more experienced Past Masters of the lodge, to give what is an important, albeit repetitive, toast. Should you have the privilege of toasting the Worshipful Master, do not fall into the trap of using the usual and tedious cliché: 'What can I say that has not already been said about our Master' or make other similar statements – they are insincere at best. Sincerity is both the most essential and, at the same time, the most difficult aspect of a speech to a Master. You need to be complimentary even when his year may have been beset with difficulties.

If you are the IPM, prepare all four or five speeches for the year from the start so that you have a theme and some continuity without repetition. You can embellish each speech as the time for its delivery approaches, with reference to events and activities that have taken place between lodge meetings. Remain aware that the Master will be responding and that he is kingpin for the night, and for the remainder of the year. Do not try to outshine him. Your experience will teach you to be sincere and modest. On those occasions when the Master is being installed for a second or even third or fourth time, a reference to his extensive experience will be acceptable. Do not hesitate to tell a light-hearted tale and make it relevant and short. One story only will suffice. Get to know the Master so that your toast will be suitable and fit in with the Master's nature and character and with which the brethren will be able to identify. It is also customary for the IPM to give the toast to the Master at the last meeting before the installation of the new Master Elect. By now a true friendship or close relationship will have developed between the two and it will be easier to be sincere. And as always, be brief.

Worshipful Master's Response

The role of a Worshipful Master of a lodge carries with it several duties and responsibilities well known to us all. It is the highest honour a lodge can bestow on any of its members.

64
I remember well telling our newly installed Master, as I greeted and congratulated him on his new office: "Well done, WM, especially since so many brethren have their eye on that seat." "Yes," he replied, "and look what I have on it."

The response by the WM at the festive board, most especially at the first dinner after installation, needs to reflect and encompass all that was prevalent at the installation ceremony in lodge: honour, trust, pride, friendship and affection. All these elements need to be manifest in a good speech, which then has to be presented with the dignity of the office of Worshipful Master. As the Master of your lodge, you are not only at its head, but you also represent the lodge in your actions and words. This is true in your own lodge and more so when visiting other lodges. You are not just a spokesman; you *are* the lodge itself, so to speak. If the lodge had a voice it would be yours, as Master. This is why dignity in your behaviour at all times, especially that reflected in your speeches, is of such importance.

You need to consider dignity both in the content of your speech as well as its delivery. The speech, as already advised, should be written out in full and delivered as if spontaneous including mandatory items that may have to be mentioned. Test yourself to see whether what you are going to say is actually true. Are you truly looking forward to becoming the Master of the lodge? Is it the fulfilment of a genuine and long-standing ambition? Have you made friends in the lodge over the years? Do your friends truly support you? And so forth. Make a list of similar questions, which will be the basis of your opening remarks in your first speech as Master. You have to reply to these questions with absolute honesty. To thine ownself be true. The answers to the questions you ask of yourself will dictate the sincerity of your speech when you are ready to deliver it. If for any reason there are problematic areas in lodge, which is the case more frequently than most brethren admit, simply keep away from the subject. Your speech at the festive board will normally follow on the Master's Song. Prepare yourself for the emotional reaction that you may not be able to control. When the song is well delivered it will bring a tear to the eye of most brethren sitting in the room. Avoid clichés in your response, though you can anticipate your reaction. Do not be afraid of being sentimental. Fear only insincerity. When totally sincere your words will flow naturally.

Your opening remarks will start with your reaction to the song; from thence let your speech reflect that this is a very special day and evening and you feel privileged and honoured. Express your genuine appreciation to the brethren who have elected you, many now good friends after years of progress together in lodge. Be very careful not to appear to be criticising or being sarcastic in any context. Do not include anything negative whatsoever in your speech. The body of what you have to say should contain both a practical plan for the year as well as a symbolic, nonetheless sincere, expression of your intention to enjoy Freemasonry at its best. In your plan for the year be brief and avoid detailed dates and timings, which will be forthcoming from the secretary in correspondence and future meetings. Let the brethren get the impression that this is going to be an active year and that you intend, through work and dedication, to reciprocate the pleasure you derive from your membership of the Craft and your own lodge in particular. When speaking of the meaning of Freemasonry, do so in a personal context. Not every brother will identify with the spiritual uplift that the Craft can give a man. Emphasise that it is your own feelings and sensations to which you refer; thus you will ensure that you do not sound arrogant or appear to talk down to the brethren.

End in a light-hearted tone and throughout you are permitted to use relevant tales that are amusing. There is no rule whatsoever that a Master's speech, no matter how solemn and important the occasion, should not be humorous. Ideally prepare all your speeches for the whole year in the knowledge that you will amend and add to them as each meeting approaches. Work on your speeches and rehearse them and you cannot but succeed. Finally, on the subject of dignity again, when you are ready to give your speech, it will all revolve around you and your actions. Ensure you look dignified, well dressed and clean-cut as already explained above. When about to speak, stand slowly and deliberately. Look every brother in the eye and project your voice, speaking clearly and loudly with the authority of your new office: the Worshipful Master of your lodge. Be confident and the brethren will be confident in you.

It is customary, at the end of your speech, to toast the Immediate Past Master. You have already had your say at some length and you should, therefore, be very brief indeed with your traditional thanks to your IPM, congratulating him on his year and thanking him for the assistance he will be rendering you during the course of the forthcoming twelve months.

Do not fail, in spite of being brief, with regard to sincerity. The year, as every Past Master will tell you, goes by with incredible speed.

 65
Time is what prevents everything from happening all at once.

Immediate Past Master's Response

The tradition of the three-pronged toast – namely IPM to Master, Master's response and toast to the IPM and the IPM's final response – is still carried out in many lodges and, if brevity is adhered to, makes a pleasant exchange. The problem is that emotions aroused at installation dinners are such that they induce long-winded and sentimental speeches, often more enjoyed by the performers than the remainder of the brethren in the room. Brief speeches are guaranteed to be successful. The IPM, when invited to respond following the Master's speech, should make a point of being very brief and modest, allowing the Master to continue in his own mode of pride and pleasure at the height of his Masonic career. A thank you and promise to allow the Master to rely on his support are sufficient words from an IPM. Definitely avoid stories or anecdotes and do not try to improve on what the Master has said. The IPM, by force of circumstance, is more experienced and will be more confident than the newly installed Master. It is therefore all the more important that he should restrain himself, and having toasted the Master appropriately at the start, should now gracefully bow out with just a few words on this second chance to speak.

Response as Master Elect

When given the opportunity to thank the Master and the brethren for the toast to you as Master Elect, your response, to a great extent, will reflect what the brethren can expect of you in the following year when you are Master. This does not refer to the content of your speech, which should make no reference whatsoever to your plans as Master. It refers to your demeanour and the way in which you deliver your response. I again emphasise that brevity will secure you respect from the start. A modest thank you and an expression of your anticipation for the year to come will be sufficient. Do not tell anecdotes. Speak, as you will do later when called upon more frequently, with confidence and cast your eye at all the brethren sitting in the dining room. Button up your jacket, stand straight and upright. Do not slouch leaning on the table. This is a very brief and simple speech: 'thank you and I look forward to it'. Do not use notes because for such a short speech it would make you appear incompetent. Most especially do not self-deprecate, avoiding at all cost any reference to the quality of the work of the Master whom you hope to emulate or, even worse, whom you think you will never be able to emulate. Like every speaker, every Master is also different from the previous. Not necessarily better and certainly not worse, just different.

Toast to the Initiate

The toast to the Initiate is the only genuinely important toast at the festive proceedings. This is the first opportunity the new member of the lodge will have to hear formal introductions to Freemasonry (outside of the tales an enterprising Tyler may have told him whilst preparing him for the ceremony of initiation). It should be left in the hands of an experienced brother rather than automatically given to the Initiate's proposer. Do not refer to the Initiate as the candidate – he is no longer a candidate. The speech has to take into account the many questions that will be going on in the head of the Initiate. Whilst it would be impossible to answer all the questions he is most probably contemplating, the speech should be oriented toward an explanation of the Craft in its historic and social setting. Once again brevity comes into play. The Initiate has already gone through a lengthy and verbose ceremony in lodge. At the festive board it would be unfair to burden him with an extended history and heavy philosophy of our Institution. Whilst both these aspects should be covered in the speech, they should be put in a light-hearted and summarised context, easily comprehensible and simplistic in its presentation.

When using dates, the year is sufficient without details of day and month. When using names and titles, a brief format will suffice without full titles, names and initials. The chronological sequence should be clear and obvious. By selecting a few key dates, the comprehensive history of the Craft can be summarised satisfactorily: 1646 the first initiation on record, that of Elias Ashmole; 1717 the foundation of organised Freemasonry, the Premier Grand Lodge of England; 1751 the foundation of a competing Grand Lodge, the Antients; 1813 the Union of the two Grand Lodges and formation of the United Grand Lodge of England. These dates indicate the antiquity of our Craft mentioned in the ritual in lodge. As to philosophy, every new brother will find that aspect in his own heart: initiation is birth and the ceremonies that will follow will open new doors for the Initiate. Make him curious and wanting to know more. Instruct him that his patience and curiosity will be amply rewarded in due course.

Most importantly, make him feel welcome amongst the brethren. Be careful not to place too much emphasis on the fact that he is *only* an entered apprentice. The danger here is that you may make him feel an outsider, which he is not. He is a fully-fledged member of the lodge and emphasis should be placed on that aspect. A suitable and historically oriented light-hearted story will be perfectly acceptable, as it will place the Initiate at ease. Welcome him into the lodge and into Masonry Universal, a concept that will become more and more apparent to him as he advances through our wonderful organisation.

Initiate's Response

Every Initiate's proposer and/or seconder to the lodge is duty bound to keep him informed of general lodge protocol and to assist and instruct him with his response to the toast given in his honour. The Initiate will often have greater problems grappling with the opening address than he has with his short speech. It will be more than sufficient for him to start his speech with 'Worshipful Master and Brethren'. This is true even in the presence of Grand Officers. Simplicity must prevail for the Initiate to feel comfortable. The Initiate's response need not consist of more than an expression of gratitude to his proposer and seconder and the brethren for receiving him into the lodge and a pledge to do his best. If he feels competent to do so briefly, the brethren will be interested to hear of his first impression as a candidate being received into the Craft. These are early days and modesty has to prevail. Avoid jokes and anecdotes.

Toast to the Visitors and Guests

Different lodges have different traditions in the selection of the lodge member who will propose the toast to the guests at dinner.

66
There is a distinct difference between a guest and a visitor, which is well exemplified when the opportunity arises to attend Wormwood Scrubs, Holloway Prison or any other similar establishment. At the end of the allotted time period, the visitors leave whilst the guests stay behind.

It is easy to remember that a brother is a visitor to the lodge and he is a guest at the festive board. In other words, a visitor is there for a temporary period of time whilst a guest's presence is by invitation and extended. In some lodges the Junior Warden traditionally gives the toast to visitors. In other lodges, the Master does so after his speech, and in some, a brother is selected at random on the evening itself, a few minutes before he is due to speak. This last circumstance should be avoided by all means. It is disrespectful to the guests, because it appears as if the toast is not of sufficient consequence to warrant preparation. It is also unfair on the selected brother, who may well be a very competent speaker, had he been given the chance to prepare himself.

A decision should normally be taken as to who the various speakers will be at the committee or Past Masters' meeting that often precedes a lodge meeting. A few days of warning is the least that should be expected unless, as stated, it is a predetermined tradition that the lodge follows. The aim of the toast, quite obviously, is to make the guests feel welcome. Make an effort, when selected to give this toast, to avoid the repetitious and cliché-filled statements of the importance of visiting etc. Instead, show pride in your lodge with a comment on its historic origins or famed members. One humorous story will suffice, as you do not wish to detract from the responder who is to follow you. Avoid commenting on the work in lodge, again this being left to the responder, should he wish to do so. At the end of the speech and before raising your glass in toast, mention the name(s) of the brethren who will be responding. Full name, rank and lodge number are appropriate.

Visitor's Reply

The response of the toast to guests and visitors is quite different from a response as a guest speaker, even if the event is similar. It is the way you are billed that makes the difference. A guest speaker will be invited and introduced as the guest for the evening. He will sit in a place of honour and be the centre of attention for the evening. This is true even though his function may essentially be to respond on behalf of the guests present. A respondent to the visitor's toast at a Masonic festive board is a casual speaker, just one part of the overall evening's proceedings. The fact that you will be responding for the guests may come to you as a total surprise as you are about to dip into your fruit salad at the end of dinner. If fortunate, you may be asked at the start of the afternoon's proceedings as to your willingness to respond. Never refuse.

Consider yourself privileged to be asked, whether impromptu or a few days in advance. The reason for this spontaneity with regard to the selection of a responder to a toast is simple. Whilst the brethren of the lodge who will be making speeches can be selected and informed at the committee meeting preceding the evening's events, the choice for a guest responder, which is normally left to the initiative of the Director of Ceremonies or the Master, is an unknown entity. It is wise to wait to see and meet with the guests present at dinner before inviting a suitable brother to honour the lodge. Do not allow the prospect of a tap on the shoulder as you await your coffee to ruin your dinner. Be prepared. Whenever invited or attending a lodge, have a speech ready with you. Use the customary niceties, avoiding remarks that are blatantly textbook comments.

Do not comment generally on the work in lodge as it is tedious and uninteresting, though to congratulate an outstanding brother because of his specific ritual work is commendable. The moment you stand to respond you are acting on behalf of every guest in the room. Your words, therefore, should reflect everything that other guests would have wished to say – express appreciation, thank your host and compliment the quality of the hospitality and of the festive board. Remain constantly sincere and if any negative thoughts occur to you, do not dare make sarcastic comments that you consider to be funny. Do not comment negatively.

67

I was disconcerted when Graham Woodrow-Taylor, an eminent Mason and my guest for the first time at my mother lodge, turned to me during the ceremony of initiation and whispered, "I must say the Master and Officers in *my* lodge really do a much better job than this, you know." When the ceremony was over, he commented that his own lodge room was far more comfortable and the acoustics were better. He then turned to me and said, "A lodge room looks so much better when the brethren are all properly clothed as they invariably are in my lodge. Your members do look a little shabbily dressed, don't they?" This tirade of criticism continued at the festive board: "That was really a poor speech that would have never taken place in my lodge," he commented. The fish was overcooked, the chicken not tender enough and the wine needed ageing. Finally, I could stand it no more. "Is there nothing at all in my lodge," I asked somewhat frustrated, "that is better than in yours?" "Oh yes, there is," he replied without hesitation. "The quality of your guests."

Light-hearted stories and anecdotes are not only welcome but can also be expected in a response by a guest. Here you can use guidelines given in chapter II, all of which apply: avoid risqué stories, avoid the subjects of sex, politics and religion. Speak clearly at everyone and be brief.

Ladies' Night

This is one of the most difficult toasts that you may be asked to make. The reason is two-fold. First, because you are speaking on behalf of every man in the room and every woman present will try to identify you and your comments with their own partners. As we well know, there are no two men that are alike, certainly not in the eyes of a wife or girlfriend. Secondly, it is difficult because whilst wishing to be honest and sincere, it is impossible to avoid the clichés associated with the sentiments you wish to express, no matter how genuine they are. How many original ways are there of saying that the ladies are gracing your festive board and that they are looking beautiful? What alternatives are there to thanking the ladies, wives and girlfriends for allowing their partners to find time for Freemasonry? And how can you express that very genuine sentiment without sounding patronising and condescending? The answer is that unless you can find a truly original approach, it is the tone of your voice, gesture and posture, namely your body language, which will have to do the work for you. You need to look immaculate, your stance and gestures modest and respectful. Select your words very carefully and the light-hearted stories must be delicate and relevant.

68
I returned home early in the morning from another lodge meeting out of town and found a piece of paper on the mantelpiece. It read: 'The day before yesterday, you came home yesterday. Yesterday you came home today. If today you come home tomorrow, you will find that I have left you . . . yesterday.'

Ironically, risqué stories, so long as they are non-sexist and inoffensive, are well accepted at mixed gatherings.

69

The wife of a dedicated Mason could no longer hold back her curiosity. She asked her eight-year-old son to spy on what daddy was doing at his Lodge of Instruction and to come and report to her. Inevitably, the brethren caught little Harold trying to listen at the door of the lodge and decided to teach him a lesson: "You wanted to know what we do," they said, "so we will make you a Mason and you will never tell our secrets to anyone." They undressed him completely, tied a piece of string around his willie and led him round the lodge three times after which they got him dressed and sent him home. "Well," said mummy when Harold returned. "What was Daddy doing?" "I cannot tell you Mummy," replied Harold, "as I am now a Mason." Mummy was not happy. "I don't know what you are talking about but there must be something you can tell me," she insisted. "That is why I sent you there.
To find out." "There is one thing I can say," said Harold pensively. "I know why girls cannot be Masons!"

Refer to your own partner and illustrate how in practice on a personal level she has assisted in your Masonic career, her patience and support, and the trials and tribulations you have been through. Use sentiments with which the female part of the audience will be able to identify. It is sincerity that will do it. Do not forget the element of brevity.

70

Early in my Masonic career, Arimz complained that I was again on my way to another Masonic meeting. I picked up the summons that had just arrived and said, "Look. It says here 'By Command of the Worshipful Master'. I have to obey." "I wish I was your Worshipful Master," she snapped. I did not comment but cannot deny the fleeting thought that we change our Worshipful Master every year.

It will be customary for one of the ladies to reply; be sure you have her name precisely and that you know how to pronounce it correctly. Obtain these details early in the evening to avoid any embarrassment. Introducing her will give you a final opportunity to express your sincere sentiments when you comment on her striking appearance, as you invite her to respond.

Other Speeches: Lady's Response

I cannot think of any reason why some ladies, particularly when Masonically inclined, should not be reading this book. Nonetheless, for those who do not do so, here are some guidelines to the partner who may wish to advise his lady on some of the protocol involved. When responding to the toast to the ladies, an important aspect is to remember that at these Ladies' Night and other mixed functions, the Worshipful Master is titled President and he

*Gran'pop replies
for the ladies*
Lawson Wood
Postcard 1920s

should be so addressed. It is also appropriate to address the assembled crowd as ladies and gentlemen rather than Brethren. This is simply because we are brethren to each other and not to non-Masons. It is, therefore, inappropriate for a lady (or any other non-Mason) to start a speech with Worshipful Master and Brethren. The Worshipful Master may be referred to as such during the speech and so may the brethren.

71
Statistics may not be reliable but they often make sense. A recent survey showed that in any mixed adult audience listening to a speech, sixty-six per cent of the audience would be thinking about sex in one form or another, irrespective of the content of the lecture. The consolation to a speaker is that no matter what you have to say, you can say it in the full confidence that two-thirds of your audience are enjoying themselves anyway.

Tyler's Toast

Whilst the toast to Absent Brethren is given as near 9.00pm as possible without comment, the Tyler's toast is a set-piece sometimes extended with some interesting variations. Here is one claimed to be a Russian version, transliterated:

> Brethren, according to ancient custom among Freemasons,
> Before rising from the festive board,
> Let us turn our thoughts to those of our brethren
> Who are scattered over the face of the earth.
>
> Let us wish solace to those who suffer;
> A speedy recovery to those in sickness;
> An improvement in their lot to those in misfortune;
> Humility to the fortunate;
> And to those who stand before the Gates of Death:
> Firmness of Heart and Peace in the Eternal East.

The Tyler will learn the toast by heart and deliver it with gusto. Rudyard Kipling's (1865-1936) poems are at times beautifully recited preceding the standard wording. 'My Mother-Lodge', composed by Kipling as part of his 'Barrack-Room Ballads' between 1889 and 1891, is undoubtedly the best known and worth quoting in full:

> There was Rundle, Station Master,
> An' Beazeley of the Rail,
> An' 'Ackman, Commissariat,
> An' Donkin' o' the Jail;
> An' Blake, Conductor-Sargent,
> Our Master twice was 'e,
> With 'im that kept the Europe-shop,
> Old Framjee Eduljee.
>
> *Outside – "Sergeant! Sir! Salute! Salaam!"*
> *Inside – "Brother," an' it doesn't do no 'arm.*
> *We met upon the Level an' we parted on the Square,*
> *An' I was Junior Deacon in my Mother-Lodge out there!*
>
> We'd Bola Nath, Accountant,
> An' Saul the Aden Jew,
> An' Din Mohammed, draughtsman
> Of the Survey Office too;
> There was Babu Chuckerbutty,
> An' Amir Singh the Sikh,
> An' Castro from the fittin'-sheds,
> The Roman Catholick!
>
> We 'and't good regalia,
> An' our Lodge was old an' bare,

But we knew the Ancient Landmarks,
An' we kep' 'em to a hair;
An' lookin' on it backwards
It often strikes me thus,
There ain't such things as infidels,
Excep', per'aps, it's us.

For monthly, after Labour,
We'd all sit down and smoke
(We dursn't give no banquits,
Lest a brother's caste were broke),
An' man on man got talkin'
Religion an' the rest,
An' every man comparin'
Of the God 'e knew the best.

So man on man got talkin',
An' not a Brother stirred
Till mornin' waked the parrots
An' that dam' brain-fever-bird;
We'd say 'twas 'ighly curious,
An' we'd all ride 'ome to bed,
With Mo'ammed, God, an' Shiva
Changin' pickets in our 'ead.

Full oft on Guv'ment service
This rovin' foot 'ath pressed,
An' bore fraternal greetin's
To the Lodges east an' west,
Accordin' as commanded
From Kohat to Singapore,
But I wish that I might see them
In my Mother-Lodge once more!

I wish that I might see them,
My brethren black an' brown,
With the trichies smellin' pleasant
An' the hog-darn passin' down;
An' the old khansamah snorin'
On the bottle-khana floor,
Like a Master in good standing
With my Mother-Lodge once more.

Outside – "Sergeant! Sir! Salute! Salaam!"
Inside – "Brother," an' it doesn't do no 'arm.
We met upon the Level an' we parted on the Square,
An' I was Junior Deacon in my Mother-lodge out there!

The Tyler is not always present at dinner and any brother may be invited to give this last and symbolic toast. Be prepared but do not volunteer if you only *think* you know it.

72 From the pens of babes

This is a selection of children's views in response to an elementary school test about the old and new testaments. They are as written out by the children without change or correction:

1. *In the first book of the bible, Guinessis. God got tired of creating the world so he took the Sabbath off.*

2. *Adam and eve were created from an apple tree. Noah's wife was Joan of Ark. Noah built an ark and the animals came on in pears.*

3. *Lots wife was a pillar of salt during the day, but a ball of fire during the night.*

4. *The Jews were a proud people and throughout history they had trouble with unsympathetic genitals.*

5. *Sampson was a strongman who let himself be led astray by a Jezebel like Delilah.*

6. *Samson slayed the philistines with the axe of the apostles.*

7. *Moses led the Jews to the red sea where they made unleavened bread which is bread without any ingredients.*

8. *The Egyptians were all drowned in the dessert. Afterwards, Moses went up to mount cyanide to get the Ten Commandments.*

9. *The first commandments was when Eve told Adam to eat the apple.*

10. *The seventh commandment is thou shalt not admit adultery.*

11. *Moses died before he ever reached Canada. Then Joshua led the Hebrews in the battle of Geritol.*

12. *The greatest miracle in the bible is when Joshua told his son to stand still and he obeyed him.*

13. *David was a Hebrew king who was skilled at playing the liar. He fought the Finkelsteins, a race of people who lived in biblical times.*

14. *Solomon, one of Davids sons, had 300 wives and 700 porcupines.*

15. *When Mary heard she was the mother of Jesus, she sang the Magna Carta.*

16. *When the three wise guys from the east side arrived they found Jesus in the manager.*

17. *Jesus was born because Mary had an immaculate contraption.*

18. *St John the blacksmith dumped water on his head.*

19. *Jesus enunciated the golden rule, which says to do unto Others before they do one to you. He also explained a man doth not live by sweat alone.*

20. *It was a miracle when Jesus rose from the dead and managed to get the tombstone off the entrance.*

21. *The people who followed the lord were called the 12 decibels.*

22. *The epistles were the wives of the apostles.*

23. *One of the oppossums was St Matthew who was also a taximan.*

24. *St Paul cavorted to Christianity; he preached holy acrimony which is another name for marriage.*

25. *Christians have only one spouse. This is called monotony.*

73 Dog for sale

When a raffle has preceded your speech, the following five words (even before Mr President, Ladies and Gentlemen) can be exceedingly effective as an opener: "I once had a dog." After a few seconds of silence during which the audience is adjusting its thinking to the deviation from the norm, continue (do not forget, at the end of the anecdote, to revert to the traditional greeting): I loved my 14-year-old Rover as did my many friends. One evening at my local pub, Michael Jones ended up offering me £500 for Rover, which I naturally refused. To my great consternation, that night, Rover passed to the Great Kennel above and I could not help contemplating the £500 that Michael had offered. Unable to sleep, I called Michael and told him that he could have Rover if he sent me a cheque for £500 in the morning. The cheque arrived the next day and I packed poor old Rover in a box and mailed the dead dog to Michael's home address. It took some months before I showed my face in the pub again, and when I did, there was Michael who greeted me with the same friendship and warmth we had always enjoyed. By the time we had finished our second pint and no mention of old Rover had been made, I could no longer hold back: "Did you receive my dog?" I enquired. "Yes, sure, thank you," said Mike about to change the subject. "But, wasn't the dog dead?" I asked. "Yes it was," replied Michael. "What did you do with it?" I ventured. "I sold it as a first prize in a raffle," was the reply. I was horrified. "A prize in a raffle?" I repeated. "Didn't anyone complain?" "Well," said Michael, "the only person who complained was the winner of the prize . . . so I gave him his £1 back."

74 Duck to water

When Norman died his wife Elsa was devastated. She was not a believer. Nonetheless, her grief got the better of her and she agreed to attend a séance session to make contact with Norman. As proceedings developed in the darkened and scented room and Norman's presence was repeatedly invoked, a voice suddenly came through: "Darling Elsa, it's me, your departed husband Norman. Please don't worry about me, my love. Everything here is great," said Norman's soothing voice. "Norman, Norman. I miss you so much. What are you doing all day?" asked Elsa. "I am up early. After breakfast I have a swim across the lake, I make love and I am back for lunch. I have an afternoon nap and swim across the lake and make love again." "But Norman," interrupted Elsa. "You weren't like that when you were here on earth." "When I was on earth," replied Norman, "I wasn't a duck, was I?"

75 Masonic football

The Royal Arch team in red were battling on against their rivals, the blue Craft team, watched by an enthusiastic group of brethren. "What's the score?" I asked, as I was about to sit down and join the spectators. "I can't tell you," replied my colleague. "It's a secret."

76 Apple millionaire

John Jacob Astor was interviewed just before sailing on the ill-fated Titanic from Southampton and was asked how he became a millionaire. "At the age of ten," he recalled, "my dad gave me the equivalent of 1 US dollar, which was quite a lot of money at the time. I bought four apples with the money and spent the night cleaning and polishing them, ready to resell them the next day. That I did and sold them at a reasonable and fair profit using the money to buy more apples. By the time I was 14, I had an apple cleaning machine, 4 wheelbarrows and two guys working for me. Then, at 18, my Uncle Benjamin died and left me his fortune. That is how I became a millionaire."

77 Midget in cannon

Adam and Eva were both just four-foot tall and in their early thirties when they decided to marry. The celebrations at the circus where they worked as a joint act went on all night. The next day, they approached an adoption agency, as they had long planned, and were interviewed by a rather sceptical consultant. "You need to be able to take care of a child, if you wish to adopt one," she said somewhat reservedly. "How do you plan to do that under the present circumstances of your employment?" "You have nothing to worry about," explained Adam. "We are the most successful act in the circus and between us earn a six-figure salary a year. We are strong and young with secure long-term employment and a healthy pension thereafter." "But you are like nomads, travelling all the time, never stationary. How will your child get an education?" asked the adoption consultant. "We will employ a full-time tutor. We will dedicate a caravan to our child who will have the best possible education." The consultant was finally moved by the sincerity and eagerness of the couple and consented to look into the possibility of allowing them to adopt. As they were about to leave the office, the consultant asked, "Incidentally, for your child, what gender would you prefer?" To which Eva replied, "It really makes no difference at all . . . as long as it fits into the cannon."

78 Egg timer

A patient was reaching a state of panic as the doctor informed him that he was terminally ill with no time left at all. "How much time do I have?" insisted the patient. "I don't know exactly," said the doctor. "Two or three minutes, perhaps?" "Good grief," cried the patient. "Can't you do anything for me?" Only one thought came to the doctor's mind, who said, "Boil you an egg . . .?"

Are you ready for the main course?

Chapter 4 summary

- Lower your sign before speaking
- Stand when taking wine
- Sit when being toasted
- Do not cross-toast
- Avoid extended opening addresses
- Speak when you have something to say
- Do not speculate or second-guess events
- Evaluate your audience
- Be sincere, dignified and avoid clichés
- Do not refer to the Initiate as the candidate
- Make the Initiate feel welcome
- Show pride in your lodge
- Avoid remarks that are textbook comments
- Do not comment on the work in lodge
- Do not use sarcasm as a substitute for humour
- Use sentiments with which a female audience will identify
- Ensure you have the correct names

Chapter 4 anecdotes

Chapter 4 additional anecdotes

CHAPTER 5

Main Course:
Lectures and talks

Blessing in Disguise

Until relatively recently, that is in the period between 1717 and the 1990s, Grand Lodge rarely, if ever, commented on any aspect of Freemasonry. It did not deem it necessary to defend or justify itself, nor issue any formal or official confirmation of its history or background outside of the *Constitutions*. The history of the Craft in the first *Constitutions* by James Anderson is notoriously fictitious and mythical. It is with some solace, therefore, that today's historian can use Masonic exposures, originally intended to attack the Craft, as a source for the Masonic activities of our forefathers in the 18th century. A report in *The Flying Post* in 1723 was the first to divulge our supposed secrets, and Prichard's *Masonry Dissected* in 1730, gave us a detailed insight into the working of the three degrees very nearly 300 years ago. It is surprisingly similar to our present ritual.

Following the formation of the Antients Grand Lodge referred to in the previous chapter, two rival and new exposures were anonymously published in 1760 and in 1762 respectively. They purported to show the ritual working of the two Grand Lodges then at loggerheads. *Three Distinct Knocks: or the Door of the Most Ancient Free-Masonry* by w****O***V****n Member of a lodge in England at this Time which saw the light of day in April 1760. The introduction states implicitly that the content is the ritual as practised at the time by the Antients. In March 1762, almost exactly two years later, *Jachin and Boaz: or An Authentic Key to the Door of Free-Masonry* was published, claiming to divulge the working of both the Moderns and the Antients. As stated, though intended to harm us, these books have turned out to be a blessing in disguise, giving today's historians a detailed insight into early Freemasonry which was previously unavailable.

Serious Subject

By the very nature of the subject, this chapter has to be on a more serious tone; however, bear in mind that knowledge is a relative matter.

79

En route to some distant destination, the long-standing chauffeur of an expert lecturer challenged his employer on their respective responsibilities.

"There you sit in the back of the car, comfortable and relaxed, snoozing at will, whilst it is me that does the real hard work, driving miles on end, concentrating on the road and traffic," the chauffeur complained. "If you think it's so easy," the professor replied, "why don't you try to deliver my lecture for me?" The chauffeur thought for a moment. "You know what, Prof?" he said with confidence. "I've heard your lecture so often by now that I reckon I could do it standing on my head." The challenge was on. They changed places in the car, and on arrival, the chauffeur was received with all the usual courtesies conferred on a guest lecturer, whilst the professor sat in the front row . . . to hear his own lecture delivered word perfect. After a hearty applause, a member of the audience stood to ask a technical question. The response from the chauffeur was immediate. "Sir, the answer to your question is so simple," said the chauffeur, pointing at the professor in the audience, "that even my driver can answer it to your satisfaction!"

Lecture vs After-dinner

Lecturing is a totally different ballgame from after-dinner speaking – a first class lecturer may well make an abysmal after-dinner speaker and vice versa. There is no reason whatsoever, however, why any one individual may not be perfectly adept at both disciplines. A lecture by its nature means that you are now tackling a new concept and you will need a more serious approach both to the content and presentation of your talk. When thinking lecture think written version; the spoken delivery version will follow through naturally. In presenting a lecture, there are, of course, logical overlaps whether you are speaking at a dinner party or addressing an overcrowded auditorium. In both cases you need to look smart, to speak clearly and comply with form and protocol required of every good speaker. There are two major differences between an after-dinner speech and a formal lecture: your approach to and preparation of your subject, and the status and expectations of your audience.

80
I have been speaking regularly at small Antique Clubs throughout England and have always been received with courtesy and friendliness. The informality and familiarity of a small membership club is refreshing. At the Ashworth Antique Collectors' Club, the President of the Society approached me as soon as I arrived. Having welcomed me with a cup of tea in her hand, she hesitated a moment and said, "This is somewhat embarrassing, Mr Beresiner, but can you tell me whether you intend charging us for your lecture?" Since I had been invited by a personal friend to address the group, I was quite happy to reply, "Not at all, I will be glad to cover my own travel expenses." "I am so glad," replied the president, "and grateful," she added. "It means that we will be able to afford a proper speaker for our next meeting."

To be a successful lecturer you need to be master of your subject. Your audience will not necessarily consist of experts, but they will have attended to learn something new. Your approach needs to take into account that you will be speaking to a captive audience whose expectations you must realise. If you don't, you will have to try harder the next time . . . if there is one!

81
This is reminiscent of the famous exchange between George Bernard Shaw and Winston Churchill. Shaw sent a telegram to Churchill just prior to the opening of *Major Barbara* in 1905, referring to Winston's move from the Conservative to the Liberal party in Parliament. He wrote: 'Have reserved two tickets for first night. Come and bring a friend, if you have one.' To which Churchill replied, 'Impossible to come to first night. Will come to second night, if there is one.'

There are only three options open to you when preparing a lecture and just two effective ways of presenting it. First, your lecture may be based on an established topic or argument and on which a third party would have already completed the research. Secondly, it may consist of a totally new theory or discovery, or, thirdly, it may be a new angle on a well-known theme. The options open to you in presenting your lecture are an ordinary verbal version or a visual presentation such as PowerPoint, slide or other illustrated means.

The Subject Matter

First and foremost, select a suitable subject and keep it simple. Whatever you decide the theme for your lecture is to be, do not complicate life. Be sure to select a subject within your scope of comprehension and, more importantly, one that you will enjoy. It is preferable to have an audience that is wide awake during your speech, and stimulated by your subject matter, than one that wakes up refreshed at the end of your talk. It is best to choose a subject with which you are familiar. To give a half hour talk or to write a 1000-word article (two pages), you have to read tens of thousands of words. A lecture will be far more successful and far easier to deliver when it constitutes only part of your knowledge on the subject. Imagine that you may need to speak for two hours or more. Now prepare a twenty-minute lecture with one hour and forty minutes of knowledge in reserve. This is not a matter of condensing or reducing the length of your talk, it is a matter of having in hand much wider knowledge well beyond what you can possibly say in the brief period that you will be speaking. That is why a subject with which you are already familiar will be helpful. If you decide to select a totally new subject, you will need to familiarise yourself with it. Read and think about it in general.

Suppose, only for convenience of thought, that your new selected subject is 'Jack the Ripper: was he a Freemason?' Much of what has been said so far will apply and is a subject you will have heard of and will be easy to understand. It is interesting and likely to be *enjoyable* to research (although that may not exactly be a suitable word for this particular topic). You may find it helpful, as I always do, to start with a children's book on the subject, because of its simplistic and factually reliable approach. It will give you a sound and clear vision of your theme and you can build your knowledge on a solid foundation. Much of the pleasure to be derived from research comes from the acquisition of new information on an ever increasingly familiar theme. Do not neglect any aspect of information that may be available on the subject. You may have the opportunity to watch a film or television documentary and the subject may appear in newspaper articles, a review of a book or a recurrent theme over an extended period. Familiarity with a subject goes beyond elements of academic research. It entails in-depth understanding and comprehension. Whilst you need not be a total expert on the subject you have selected, you will need a solid background to be sure that your lecture will be well received and that you maintain the respect afforded to a knowledgeable lecturer.

82
It seems to me that the older I get, the better I used to be. On the other hand, age is only important if you are a bottle of wine. In any case we don't stop playing because we get old – we get old because we stop playing.

An Established Story

Should you choose, perfectly legitimately, to use a well-known theme or someone else's ideas for your lecture, make sure that it is abundantly clear to all concerned that you are not expounding new concepts or theories and that your selected subject is someone else's work. It may be a Dickensian novel or a summary of Plato's Philosophy of Science. You may select a recently published paper in one of the transactions of the research lodges in England. Do not expose yourself to any comment or criticism on the grounds that you misled anyone into thinking yours was original material.

83
Oscar Wilde may have had something similar in mind when he stated 'It is perfectly monstrous the way people go about nowadays saying things against one, behind one's back, that are absolutely and entirely true.'

It is worth repeating that it is essential, even when speaking on an established theme, to have a thorough knowledge of the subject, beyond the scope and limitations of a half-hour talk. If, on the other hand, you want to be original – which is necessary, for instance, when preparing a new lecture for a research lodge – then there are only two venues open to you: it has to be either a totally new concept or discovery or a totally new angle to an already established and researched theme. This principle applies to Freemasonry in particular and, to a great extent, to other fields of endeavour.

New Theory

You may be fortunate enough to have come across some previously unknown document or Masonic object or you may have your own original thoughts, philosophies and ideas, even ideals, about Freemasonry. You can develop any of these into a lecture, the content of which will be *original* material. Your chosen theme has to be clear-cut and specific. Do spend time and make an effort to compose a title that will reflect the content of your speech. Once you have decided on your theme, your next priority is to trace, as far as possible, all the available material already published on your chosen topic.

Plagiarism

Plagiarism goes beyond the dangerous quip, that to use one source is plagiarism, but to use two is research. You are at liberty, indeed you need to use other sources to clarify and better formulate your own theories and findings. Keep a detailed record of all articles, publications and references that you find, such as detailed records, author, title, publisher and date. Your research may even extend to the page number of the work referred to when quoting statements or making a particularly important point. It is how you use these sources that touches on that delicate area of plagiarism and it is essential for you to acknowledge the sources you have used. You do so by reference, giving the details of the sources you have used. This will also allow the readers of the written version of your paper to distinguish your own work from that of your sources. Whenever you read or research material, make sure that you include in your own notes the full publication details of each work that you have read. All this clearly applies to the written versions of your lecture, which you may very well be in a position to publish. Should you pursue that possibility, you will find that there are different systems of referencing and rich literature explaining referencing conventions.

Research

The word 'research' does not convey the true significance of the term – it implies that you can just go and do some *research*. That is not the case. Research does not take place as an isolated activity; it is part of a fairly lengthy process through which you have to go, without options. Shortcuts are possible but to your detriment and not really worthwhile. As soon as you become competent, you will regret the use of shortcuts and learn that you will have to start all over again. There is no reason why you should not seek assistance with researchers but keep total control of the information obtained.

Ceremony, Pomp and Formality
Anon caricature c1810 (Guildhall)

84
Do not use the hook and eye method when wanting to get things done. Do them yourself. The hook and eye method is when you think to yourself 'who can I get to do this and who can I get to do that?'

It is essential that you first establish your discovery as a genuine find and previously unpublished. To do this you need to source out as much available information as you can lay your hands on. Start with the obvious: Masonic dictionaries and works of reference. Two such books of reference I can immediately recommend are the late Harry Carr's *The Freemason at Work*, first published in 1976, and of which revised and new editions are available, and the somewhat more cumbersome tome *Gould's History of Freemasonry* which has been published in many and varied editions since 1886 in three, four and six volumes. It is relatively expensive and reasonably readily available in second-hand and some Masonic bookshops. Every Masonic library will have a copy and it is the most comprehensive history of Freemasonry so far published. Another smaller book, John Hamill's *The Craft* published by Ian Allan Publishing, is intended as much for Freemasons as it is for the neophyte and the uninitiated. It is refreshingly straightforward, easy to follow, to understand and, most importantly, factually reliable. Encyclopaedias and dictionaries will list subject matters in alphabetic order. They are plentiful and easy to use.

The ones that quickly come to mind are John Lane's *Masonic Records 1717-1894*. A facsimile edition was published a few years ago. This is an essential tool for finding information about lodges under the English Constitution that existed between 1717 and 1894. Frederick Smyth's *A Reference For Freemasons*, published by QC lodge in 1998, is a most reliable and useful volume. A more difficult book to find at present is *10,000 Famous Freemasons* by William Denslow published in four volumes by Macoy. It is not as large and cumbersome as it sounds. The four volumes usually come in their own protective box case. Albert G. Mackey's *Revised Encyclopaedia of Freemasonry*, first published in the USA in 1873 with more modern editions into the 1950s and later, is still available. It is probably the best known of the various encyclopaedias. There is need for caution as not all the publications above are entirely and absolutely reliable with their facts. Always obtain a secondary confirmation. Having started your sourcing, you will find that every source you identify leads you on to another one, sometimes to private publications and pamphlets as well as magazine or newspaper articles. Follow through and verify each lead as far as practicable.

Transactions & Newspapers

Having completed your initial search in dictionaries and the like, you now need to have a closer look at papers that may have been published in the transactions of the various Masonic research lodges. The three most prominent are: *Ars Quatuor Coronatorum* (AQC); the transactions of the Quatuor Coronati Lodge in London, universally accepted as the Premier Lodge of research worldwide; Research lodges in Leicester and Manchester. AQC predominates because the papers presented in open lodge are published with written comments by readers. This secondary source ensures that errors are rectified and it often adds information or a new aspect to the body of the paper presented. Combined with the article, the comments are a useful and important source for the researcher. Do not hesitate to make contact, or better still, visit the Library and Museum of Freemasonry in Great Queen Street, London, when you require verification or more detailed information. Our library has an index of the Quarterly Communications of the United Grand Lodge of England covering volumes 1869 to date. Previous volumes have not been indexed.

Other magazines and journals should also be sourced, including the transactions of the many international lodges of research. Unfortunately, indexes are not always available for long-running magazines and journals but your research can benefit from the complete sets of Masonic transactions on DVD. Here digital searching becomes very easy. Some organisations choose to publish their material on websites accessible through the Internet, although several sites will require you to register in order to gain access to material. No matter how predominantly Masonic your theme may be, do not get trapped within the limited confines of a Masonic framework.

Freemasonry has not existed or survived in an historic vacuum; it is very much part of a social and political environment developing and prospering over a period of several centuries. You need to expand your horizons and look outside and beyond the Masonic structure. Initially make use of non-Masonic dictionaries and encyclopaedias. The voluminous *Dictionary of National Biography* is an essential and important source whenever personalities and individuals are included in your research work. You will need to find other sources related to your theme. The excellent collection of newspapers belonging to the British Library is a very important primary source of information and can be consulted in the Newspaper Reading Rooms in Colindale, North West London. This national archive collection consists of British and overseas newspapers and includes popular magazines and periodicals of all periods.

Write Out your Lecture in Full

It is essential for you to prepare in writing the paper or lecture you are planning to give. This will serve two purposes: preparation of your lecture for your own reference, and a written version for deposit with the minutes or other records kept by the lodge or institution that you are addressing. Having listed your basic bibliography, and presumably made notes for your own reference, you are ready to begin to place on paper a framework within which your article will finally fit as near perfectly as possible. Start with a chronology of relevant dates, entering against each year a summarised single line description of the event you are recording. Use an unlimited number of subtitles, which will serve you both as an index when you come across new material and allow you to keep a logical sequence to your paper. You will be able to move whole paragraphs from one section to another as the article takes shape. The subtitles can be reduced or deleted when your final draft is ready.

When you come across a source given by another author, check it out. Go to the sources cited and confirm the details – you will be amazed to find how many sources are incorrectly quoted. This is either by simple error or because sources referred to over an extended period have been repeated without checking, perpetuating the same errors over and over again. The written version of your paper needs to be accurate. For every hour you dedicate to writing your paper, apply an equal amount of time to check facts, figures, spelling, dates and sources. For example, the BBC allocates one-hour of research time for every minute spoken on air. Although the written version of your paper may not be intended for publication, it will still constitute a source of reference to anyone who may wish to consult or study your words more carefully. The leeway and licence you have in the verbal delivery version of your speech does not extend to the written one. You will need a bibliography to guide the reader and you must cite the documents that you have used.

After your paper is written out in full, you can convert it to a delivery version by reducing it to a manageable size on cards which can be used when speaking. Your lecture, that is the verbal presentation of your written paper, should always be shorter than you plan. It will consist of three parts: a start with a light-hearted story, a middle that will contain the body of what you have to say, and an end which will be a very short summary with an appropriate conclusion. Do not hesitate to use light-hearted stories no matter how serious your subject (or the audience) may be.

85

I remember an original welcome to a speech when the host who introduced me stood, faced the audience and said, "Ladies and gentlemen, you are almost welcome to this lecture . . ." He stopped, coughed and slightly embarrassed said, "I am so sorry, I will start again. Ladies and gentlemen, you are all most welcome to this lecture . . ."

Primary Sources

A primary source is the first possible available source, namely the actual original item itself, normally a manuscript but perhaps printed matter such as a newspaper report. A contemporary commentator will qualify as a primary source when his own words, as first expressed, are accessible. The primary source no longer applies the moment we use someone who heard or quotes the original source. That is a secondary source. Thus James Anderson's second 1738 edition of the *Constitutions* is considered to be a primary source, because no other earlier information is available. It gives us detailed information on the activities of Grand Lodge between 1717 and 1723. After that date, the minutes, begun in the same year, take over. Incidentally, the production by Anderson of the first and second *Constitutions* in 1723 and 1738 respectively was a private venture – therefore, these *Constitutions* were not the official publications of the Grand Lodge of England. It should also be noted that Anderson's *Constitutions* are not seen as a reliable source and are far from being realistic.

However, the 1738 records are the only available and first source of the events that took place two decades earlier. Similarly, newspaper reports and the content of Masonic periodicals reporting on events as they occur, daily or weekly, are a primary source. The most useful and comprehensive, in Masonic terms, is the weekly *The Freemason* (1869-1957) which is blessed with an invaluable index. Obviously, primary sources are not always available but an effort should be made to trace the primary source, if at all possible, when making statements on matters of consequence and importance. In Masonic research we are fortunate in England to have available to us the resources of the Library and Museum of Freemasonry in Great Queen Street, London. Bear in mind that ours is a closed access, reference only library, open 10.00am to 5.00pm Monday to Friday. There are approximately 46,000 books on the subject of Freemasonry with the larger part of the collection devoted to English Freemasonry. There are, of course, a considerable number of books on Freemasonry in other countries as well as a large selection of related books. It is necessary for all visitors to the library to register. The enhanced website *www.freemasonry.london.museum* allows easy access to all material including bibliographies, archives and other facilities. If you want to discover something new, keep an eye open. There is a great deal of material out there.

New Angle

The third option in selecting a theme is to choose a well-known and accepted theory, with which everyone is already familiar and look at it from a different angle. An example is a Masonic biography of a personality who was a Freemason or a famous Freemason. There is a distinct difference between the two: men of stature such as Winston Churchill, the Duke of Wellington, George Washington, to name just three, were famous men whose Masonic activities did not contribute to their fame. They also happened to be members of the Craft. This is not the same as famous Freemasons such as James Anderson, Laurence Dermott, Thomas Dunckerley – all of whom would have passed into oblivion but for their involvement in Freemasonry. In both cases written material will be available on every man of consequence who was a Freemason.

You can select and choose one individual and see whether you can approach his biography from an angle that is different and original. First, read as much about your subject as you can and keep an open mind for possible investigation. Do not rely only on quoted references but search the background of anyone whose name is mentioned associated with your subject, and endeavour to discover his background and connections. Get in touch with schools, universities and institutions with which your subject was associated; you may be pleasantly surprised by what you discover. When reading Masonic literature or listening to a lecture, keep in mind material that is being presented as a source for future reference. There are many unanswered questions directly relating to published historical articles and they can be the basis for new research.

Rehearse, Rehearse, Rehearse

When preparing for the delivery of your lecture, you cannot rehearse too many times. You should have formal rehearsals in the privacy of your home and, as the time for your lecture approaches, go through headings, dates and names. When ready for a full rehearsal at home, you will need to time yourself. Stand in front of a full-size mirror, which will allow you to observe and improve your gestures and stance, and speak aloud at the pitch that you know you will need in the hall where your lecture is due to be delivered. Leave nothing to chance. Concentrate on the links that join up your light-hearted anecdotes, which incidentally should not be incorporated into the written version of your paper, with the body of your theme. Do not presume that you will remember a link or that it will come to you naturally. A link is essential to ensure continuity, and as long as you have continuity, your audience will not be distracted. Nothing should distract your audience from giving you their full and absolute attention. This is why the dress code is so important. If you look odd or untidy, if you gesticulate or move about excessively, if you lose track of what you are saying and so forth, your audience may lose interest.

86
A good audience mix is one that consists of young, middle-aged and 'don't you look well' men and women.

Gestures

You must have total control of the movement of your hands and arms whilst you are speaking. If you use a podium, you are to some extent hidden from the audience; however, you should still place both hands on the podium when speaking. If given the freedom to move about, which is by far preferable and only possible when you have mastered the art of speaking without notes, make good use of the space you allocate yourself for motion. Place yourself in the centre facing everyone and not on one side of the stage. Do not step more than one or two metres in any one direction, or if you do so, do it infrequently. For most of the time, stand firm, hands clasped in front or placed behind you. Release your hands or change their positioning only when emphasising a point. Standing in front of your audience allows you to express points with your whole body, not just your hands. For instance, when asking a question, rhetorical or practical, you should take a step forward lightly inclining your body as you hypothetically enquire: can anyone of you answer without qualm? Similarly when expressing doubt, disbelief or difficulties, you can do so taking a step or leaning back as you state: it will not happen in my lifetime! These should serve as examples of body language which you should have previously practised and which will later come more naturally as you progress and become more experienced. Use your hands for emphasis only when standing still – to move about and gesticulate will definitely distract the listener. At this stage you may wish to read through the advice given in chapters II and III, as all the same elements now apply with regards to the delivery of your lecture.

Make Yourself Known

Also applicable are the points already made; that you should familiarise yourself with the venue, arrive early and so forth. There is now the added element of making yourself known to the organisers of your lecture.

A well-fed brother and gentleman
Humphrey c1800

In lodge, approach the secretary first so that he is aware of your arrival and can take that concern off his mind as he concentrates on other preparations. Ask to be introduced to the Director of Ceremonies and inform him of the position from which you intend to lecture. In a lodge room I suggest that you speak from the left of the Senior Warden – this allows you to face the Master and dignitaries present in the East. It will also allow a few seconds, as you walk from East to West, to take deep breaths and to build a sense of anticipation whilst the brethren observe you positioning yourself. As a guest speaker, irrespective of your rank, you should under normal circumstances be invited to sit on the Master's right. If a Provincial Grand Master or a Visiting Grand Officer is present on official business, they take precedence over you though many senior brethren will often concede their seat to a recognised speaker. It is not your choice as to where you are seated – wait until the DC instructs you and takes you to your seat. You will need to co-ordinate with the DC the procedure he wishes to adopt when it is your turn to speak.

When you have been introduced by the Master, stand up, salute him and ask his permission to address the brethren from the West. The DC will now approach and accompany you to your spot, earlier indicated to him. Wait for the DC to return to his seat, salute again and start your lecture. In some lodges where a point is made of not being formal in any way, you may be seated amongst the brethren and make your own way to the West when called to speak by the Master. Follow whatever procedure is dictated to you. You are a guest and modesty and dignified demeanour will serve you best. When you finish your talk, salute the Master and wait for the DC to return you to your seat if so pre-arranged, or make your way back. Do the same on occasions when the Master may allow questions. Never refuse to answer questions. Return to your seat, sit down and then stand to respond to any questions asked. Always repeat the question that is asked before responding as this will make sure that everybody has heard the question clearly and will give you time to formulate an appropriate response. Keep your responses to questions brief and succinct. Do not give a second lecture in response to a question. Do not be afraid to say 'I don't know'. It is by far preferable than mumbling an unsuitable explanation, which may well be recognised by your audience to be totally inappropriate.

No Notes is Best

As previously mentioned on several occasions, the ability not to use notes is only a matter of practice and confidence. It is not as difficult as many speakers fear and is by far the most efficient way of delivering a lecture or any other speech. Start early in your speaking career to learn your subject, even when using notes. Gradually the notes in your hand should become superfluous and only for use as reference or when making a quote. Under no circumstances should you read out your lecture from written pages – it is important that you should not do so as you will lose your status as a speaker if you read out your own paper verbatim. The only time that a paper can be legitimately read out in full from the text is when someone is delivering a lecture on behalf of a speaker unable to attend in person. Otherwise, notes should only be used as a support whilst you speak, observing your audience and occasionally glancing at your notes, not the other way round. Once more, keep the delivery version of your lecture short. Between 20 minutes to half an hour is more than adequate. There is no limit to the length of the written version, which will be available to members of your audience if interested.

A short lecture will let your audience absorb what you have had to say and allow time for questions, where appropriate, to enable you to amplify your thoughts. Ensure your apron and collar or sash, if applicable, sit well on your body as your appearance is an indication of your respect for those you are addressing. Keep eye contact with all of the audience. Look at individual members of your audience in the eye and hold their attention. Look around you, especially in lodges where there may be brethren sitting behind the Senior Warden's chair, thus out of your range of vision. Once or twice during the lecture, turn all the way back to acknowledge them. Do not, however, speak when looking round. Wait till you face the whole of your audience before continuing to speak. Do not fix your gaze at only the Master or the brethren seated in the East. Speak loudly, clearly, slowly and deliberately. Do not change the tempo of your voice, especially if you realise that you may be running beyond the allocated time. Do not worry about forgetting or leaving out facts or figures. Never apologise or backtrack.

PowerPoint or Slide Presentation

When your lecture is to be accompanied by illustrations, never use sheets of paper, photographs or other material to be passed around the room – it is the most ineffective and distracting thing you can do. Your audience, except for the one person with your illustration in hand, will not know what you are referring to. By the time the illustration finally gets to them, you will have been speaking about something else, which they will not understand, or, worse still, not be listening at all as they have been distracted by an insignificant piece of paper. If you need to use such an illustration, display it in front of the audience, even when it will obviously not be within easy sight of those sitting too far back.

With regard to your illustrated presentation, there is no difference whether you use a slide projector or a computer. In addition to the various points already made relevant to speaking in general, it is important when using illustrations on a screen, to allow the images to appear as a background to your lecture and not a substitute for it. The slides should support, illustrate and enhance a lecture, not replace it. Ideally, you should be able to give the identical illustrated lecture without slides, having only to omit references to the images that would have otherwise appeared on the screen. There are obvious exceptions where, for instance, the slide illustrates a graph or an image that is an integral part of the lecture and essential for the audience to understand your explanation. Should anything go wrong with your equipment, not relying on the images will enable you to carry on speaking without concern.

When using any audio-visual equipment, whether a tape recorder to convey music or a television screen to illustrate a film sequence, ensure the availability of equipment at the venue where you will be speaking. Attend the lecture room well in advance of the meeting and ensure that the equipment you are going to use is in good order. You will need to determine the location of the power points and the light switches. Never switch off all the lights when making your presentation – it is not necessary and will remove both your ability to see your audience and prevent them from seeing you. You need to see your audience and monitor their response in order to judge how you are doing. Ideally, it is preferable for the area immediately above the screen to be dark and the rest of the room to be lit with dimmed lights but not switched off. You need to position your screen in relation to the projector allowing you space to stand by the screen and face the audience. This will also enable you to point out any relevant aspects of the image on the screen.

Through the auspices of the secretary or DC, organise a Steward or some other brother to assist you to set up your equipment. Before you start to speak, and whilst all the lights are still on, project one slide onto the screen to ensure everyone is within visual range. Have someone assist with the lighting, asking that they should wait for your instruction and not take their own initiative. Start your introduction and any light-hearted anecdotes before the lights are lowered. Do not be concerned, when using slides, that you will not be able to see your notes: the slides themselves will serve as excellent memory triggers and are a very good substitute for notes. If you can, learn the sequence of the slides and you will not need notes. When addressing the audience from the side of the screen, do not face the screen when speaking. If you need to look at an image on the screen, stop talking and turn to the audience again before continuing to speak. In spite of the darkened room, behave throughout as if it is fully lit. Do not think that you can break the many rules expounded: keep eye contact with your audience, do not gesticulate, look presentable and speak loudly and clearly.

This is the end of instructions on speaking and lecturing.

---

87 Smith & Smith
Business was not so good for Yehezkel Yankelevitch and Ephraim Rabinovitch. They were sitting in armchairs outside their deserted furniture shop when Ephraim had a brilliant idea. He took off and returned with stepladders, a brush and paint and declared, "I have changed my name to Smith." He immediately proceeded to change the sign above the shop, which now read YANKELEVITCH & SMITH in big, bold letters. Yehezkel liked the idea and did exactly the same; the sign now read SMITH & SMITH. They sat expectantly waiting for new business when the phone rang. "Is that Smith and Smith?" enquired a voice at the other end of the line. "Yes, this is Smith and Smith," replied Ephraim in anticipation. "Can I speak with Mr Smith, please?" asked the caller. "Which one?" Ephraim replied. "Yankelevitch or Rabinovitch?"

88 How to hug
I must have been 12 or so when I dared to enter the first adult bookshop and surreptitiously purchased a large volume titled *How to Hug*. Back home, locked in my bedroom, I took out the book to discover that I had purchased volume eight of the *Encyclopaedia Britannica*.

89 Doctors tell me nothing
The helpful receptionist answered the telephone enquiry at the Royal National Orthopaedic Hospital in Stanmore, regarding Mr Haythornethwaite in the Coleman Ward. He was doing fine after the operation. He would probably be released on the Wednesday. He was not likely to need to return to the hospital. "Who is this speaking?" finally asked the receptionist. "It is me, Mr Haythornethwaite, in the Coleman Ward. The doctors won't tell me a thing."

90 Sleepy ritual
Our newly elected Master announced that he had devised a method of learning the whole of the ritual of the three degrees without effort and be word perfect. Over a period of a few weeks, he placed recording tapes (without the key words, of course) under his pillow before going to sleep and played them through the night. "Does it really work?" I asked. "It works great," he announced. "I know all three degrees word perfect . . . except that I can only recite them when asleep."

Chapter 5 summary

- When thinking *lecture* think *written*
- Select a suitable subject and keep it simple
- Keep knowledge in reserve
- Do not expose yourself to criticism
- Compose a title that will reflect the content
- Acknowledge your sources
- Do not take shortcuts
- Write out your lecture in full
- Check out quoted sources
- You cannot rehearse too many times
- Do not presume you will remember your links
- Control the movement of your hands and arms
- Make yourself known to the organisers
- No notes is best
- Never apologise or backtrack
- Never pass illustrations round the room
- Slides should support a lecture, not replace it
- Never switch off all the lights
- Do not face the screen when speaking
- Keep eye contact with your audience

Chapter 5 anecdotes

Chapter 5 additional anecdotes

After the Festive Board
Hogarth 'Times of Day' 1738 (YB)

CHAPTER 6

Desserts & Coffee:
Surprise and initiative

Hogarth et al

In 1736, William Hogarth (1697-1764), the greatest English satirical artist and a Freemason, found himself at loggerheads with one Sir Thomas de Veil (1684-1746), a Justice of the Peace and a member of the lodge meeting at the Vine Tavern, Holborn, which Hogarth also frequented. The antagonism between the two led to the best known of all of Hogarth's Masonic prints, namely *Night*, one of a set of four prints collectively titled *Times of Day,* of which *Night* was the fourth. The four prints are to be seen in context as they tell a story of a day's happenings in the streets of London. The last print reflects the not uncommon late night celebrations in the back streets of the city. Freemasonry, identified as a dining and drinking club, falls into this bracket of revelry. Thomas de Veil, wearing his Master's collar and jewel, is blatantly drunk, following a Masonic evening and festive board. He is being helped home, as would be the custom, by the Grand Tyler at the time, identified as Andrew Montgomery, 'Garder of ye Grand Lodge'.

The print, typical of Hogarth's work, is filled with detail and innuendo. In the background is the sign of the Rummer and Grape Tavern in what is now Northumberland Avenue. There is considerable significance to the scene in which the content of a chamber pot is being poured onto de Veil's head. It is a commentary and gibe at de Veil, who was involved in the legislation banning the popular trade in gin. On one well-publicised occasion, the unfortunate de Veil, whilst testing the liquid content of a bottle in a tavern, inadvertently gulped down a mouthful of urine, placed there by customers aware of his pending visit. De Veil, known to be a heavy drinker and womaniser, was nonetheless quite an extraordinary character. He had had no fewer than four wives and 25 children. He had fought in the War of the Spanish Succession, and when appointed Stipendiary Magistrate in 1738, acted decisively and with passion. Hogarth's humiliating depiction of his fellow Mason went beyond any consideration of fraternal loyalty.

A Masonic festive board set up, though disturbed by events, is also depicted in the well-known print headed *The Free-Masons Surpriz'd Or The Secret Discover'd*. It is a quaint light-hearted print, commonly referred to as 'Old Molly' and published by Robert Sayer in 1752. The sub-title is self-explanatory: 'A True Tale from a Masons lodge in Canterbury'. The print is almost educational, showing us interesting aspects of contemporary customs and mannerisms. The long aprons and use of the buttonhole, the firing glasses and clay pipes on the table are all reminiscent of the early days of Freemasonry.

 91

The explanatory couplets at the base of the print read as follows:

The Chamber Maid, Moll, a Girl very fat,
Lay hid in the Garrett as shy as a Cat;
To find out the Secret of Masons below,
Which no one can tell, & themselves do not know,
Moll happen'd to slip, & the Ceiling broke thro,
And hung in the posture you have in your View;
Which freightn'd the masons, tho doing no Evil,
Who stoutly cried out The Devil! The Devil!
With phiz white as Apron, the Masons ran down;
And call'd up the Parson, his Clerk, & the Town;
To lay the poor Devil thus pendant above,
Who instead of Old Nick, spy'd the Temple of Love.

Come all prying Lasses take warning by Moll,
The subject of this, the Print, and the Droll,
To get at a Secret which ne'er can be known
By an unlucky Slip She discover'd her own;
And the Masons may learn without touching hoops
That some of their Brothers are not Nincumpoops
That Parsons and Clerk, with their sanctified Faces,
Had a peep at Molls Rouser, & just so the Case is.

Whilst on the subject of Masonic prints, a third well-known Masonic caricature cannot remain unmentioned. The engraved print is dated 21 November 1786 and shows the inside of a lodge room. It has dual French and English text and is titled *A Masonic Anecdote – Anecdote Maçonique* (reproduced on the front cover). A line of text states: 'Designed by a brother Mason a Witness to the Scene'. It has been attributed, with some reservation, to James Gilray (1757-1815) who was not a Freemason. The print is very much in the style of this most famous satirical artist and engraver, and was published in London by Hannah Humphrey, the leading print-seller at the time. The subject matter of the print is of historic interest. It refers to Count Cagliostro (1743-1795) also known by his real name of Joseph Balsamo, the Italian Freemason who died disgraced in prison. Cagliostro has been designated the greatest Masonic charlatan of all time. He was imprisoned by the Inquisition for criminal acts associated with his Masonic activities. Cagliostro had also nominated himself the

The Free-Masons Surpriz'd Or The Secret Discover'd
Sayer caricature 1752

Grand Kophte of the Egyptian Rite of Freemasonry and invented numerous degrees: up to 96 for one of his orders, charging a fee for each degree. He died in prison in San Leone, Italy, in 1795. The print records Cagliostro's visit to the lodge of Antiquity No 1 (now No 2) in London on 1 November 1786. Cagliostro and four colleagues from the Loge L'Espéreance No. 369 are seated together whilst Bro Richard Marsh MP, exposes them as charlatans. The Worshipful Master, brother Barker, is seated at the table and the Chevalier Ruspini can be seen in the background. The text, in rhyme, explains and describes how they were expelled in disgrace from the lodge.

Never Refuse

Having taken into account everything said so far in the first five chapters of this book, never refuse an invitation to speak.

92
Sven Stephenson was a permanent guest at the City of London Luncheon Club and with every opportunity that he had to speak, he did so, often with excessive enthusiasm. His eagerness to join the dining club was apparent to all and sundry but he could not find a single member to sponsor his membership application. Finally, after many visits and much persuasion, he succeeded in obtaining a proposer and seconder. On the day of his

election,

Stephenson was asked to leave the room for a few minutes whilst the vote was to be taken. On his return to the dining room, the President addressed him sombrely: "I am very sorry, Mr Stephenson, but I have to inform you that all 52 votes were against you." "How is that possible?" asked a genuinely dismayed Sven. "There are only 50 members present." "Yes," replied the President, "but two of the waiters don't like you either."

You will never know what opportunity may present itself. You may be invited to give an after-dinner speech, or asked to introduce or thank another speaker, or give a fully-fledged lecture. It makes no difference how experienced you are, especially if you have purchased this book and have read this far, then you are definitely ready to accept any invitation to speak. I would venture to suggest, so long as this book was not a gift and you did not start it from the end, that you should actively create the opportunity to speak.

It was under those very same circumstances that I started my lecturing career. It was my friend, the late and lamented Bro Henry Clipp, in whose footsteps I followed as secretary of my mother lodge, that encouraged and supported me to venture into Masonic speaking. He gave me the opportunity to present my very first illustrated talk on Masonic coins to the members of the lodge. Bro Eric Beecham, whose friendship I value to this day, came to my home, listened to me rehearse as well as guiding me; it gave me the confidence every new speaker needs. From the moment I started speaking in lodge, surrounded by dozens of familiar, warm and friendly faces, I relaxed. I was soon invited to give lectures in other lodges, though ironically, I never again had the opportunity to do so in my own mother lodge – there must be a lesson to be learned there.

93
The Chairman of the Lodge Committee who, by tradition, happens to be the Senior Warden in my lodge, was hospitalised and unable to attend the committee meeting. In the morning he was pleased to receive a get-well message from the secretary, which read 'The committee took a decision to express their sincere good wishes for a speedy and complete recovery. Six in favour, three against, one abstention.'

Your mother lodge is most definitely a good starting point. You will have already made your maiden speech and no doubt had the opportunity to give one or more toasts. You are now in a position to take the initiative. Do not wait for an invitation. Approach the lodge committee through the secretary requesting the opportunity to present your lecture in lodge. Your lecture should be complete and ready to be delivered *before* you approach the committee. You will also need to give them a brief, though clear synopsis of your talk and its length. Keep your first lecture brief. In your own lodge, it will not be required to explain that this is your first effort as every brother will have been made aware of the fact. If the urge is irresistible, by way of an introduction and without apology, explain the circumstances that led you to prepare and present the talk and your future plans. Do not apologise or justify your actions. Not to apologise is an important habit to get into from the very start – an apology will either come through as false modesty or an unnecessary distraction. Why attract attention to your weakness? Never apologise.

The alternative to your mother lodge is a private function: a group of friends and colleagues to whom you can make your first presentation in private. Do not expect to acquire total knowledge of your subject as the more you learn the more you will realise how little you know. There is no point in refusing an invitation whilst waiting to be better prepared. You will always have a need to be better prepared no matter how experienced you become and how often you give the very same talk. You have to start sometime, and to start by taking the initiative and not refusing the first time you are invited to speak will be wise. Be very cautious and think again if you are about to stand and speak with the confidence of a man who knows everything there is to be known on the subject. There is no such genius . . .

I would not encourage you to aggressively pursue invitations to speak at lodges or after dinner, as that will be an imposition: an institution such as ours, that is essentially polite and considerate would not refuse you even when it may be inconvenient. I would recommend that you register your name on the list of speakers maintained by the London Grand Rank Association and/or the equivalent Provincial Offices. Keep your ears open for an opportunity to present itself – when you hear that a lodge has no work and is looking for something to do or someone to speak, offering your services is perfectly acceptable. You must be confident in yourself, confident that you will not let down either yourself or the audience and the fact that you are new to the speakers' circuit will not matter. Every speaker without exception, no matter how talented and popular now, was once a beginner like you.

94

At a military lodge in Ireland, the brethren were delighted that their Commander in Chief had agreed to join the Craft. At the initiation ceremony, the two deacons responsible for the colonel being initiated were both ordinary soldiers in the unit. The secretary chose to record this historic event in the minutes as 'one of those rare occasions when the candidate was led around the lodge by his privates'.

Be Prepared

When invited to dine or attend a venue where speeches are on the agenda such as Masonic festive boards or a social club dinner, always have a short speech ready. Be on time or even early.

95

I was late to a meeting because of faulty traffic lights at a junction not far from my venue. A policeman was directing the traffic and I must have lost concentration when he signalled me to move on. I did not budge, my mind on other things. After signalling me two or three times to move forward, the policeman finally approached my car, knocked on the window which I lowered and said, "Excuse me sir, are you waiting for me to turn green?"

As you make a name for yourself, you will find that you are asked to speak more often than you would expect. A ready-made speech in your pocket, should you be approached, will need last moment improvisation to fit the occasion. The event will dictate the improvisation that you should apply. You have to use some ingenuity and imagination, to make your speech appear both spontaneous and relevant. Light-hearted stories and anecdotes are fine and essential but they have to be interspersed with some serious and relevant comments to give your speech weight. There are many options open to you; however, you must concentrate on one theme, as there is no advantage to be gained by jumping from one theme to another. If spontaneously invited, you are not likely to be expected to speak for more than a few minutes, perhaps five at the very most. This means that you can select one subject only, outside the anecdotes that you will be relating, and fill your time without deviation from that specific theme. For instance, you may choose a topic of some non-political or non-religious news item of consequence, possibly a celebration of some event or other. You can even select to speak about a neighbour at dinner (seriously, that is) who may have triggered your memory during the conversation you enjoyed with him. I have always found my dad, Lazi, an excellent subject because I could be absolutely truthful about him. He was a grand old man.

96

We were on our way to a meeting by Underground when the train jolted and a pretty woman passenger landed on my dad's lap. Neither of them moved for a few moments until my dad quipped, "Would you mind standing up, young lady. I am not as old as I thought I was."

Until he became a Freemason at the age of 78, his total daily activity consisted of the short drive from home to the bridge club and the drive back many hours later. He became so enchanted by the Craft, however, that he insisted on accompanying me to all my lectures no matter how distant from home. As we drove hour after hour, he insisted that I should rehearse my lectures aloud, and by the time we arrived at our destination, he was genuinely informed of the essence of my speech. A father, however, will always remain a father. When it was time for questions after my lecture at a lodge in Manchester, my father was the first to put his hand up. After our journey in the car, I presumed that he had something on his mind. "Yes, Lazi?" I enquired. "Can we please have the lights on," he asked, "so that we can see you better?"

Quote Freely

When taking the initiative or having been invited at the last moment to speak at a function, do remember that you are not a stand-up comedian. Your task as an after-dinner speaker is far more dignified. You are not expected to, and you should not, reel off joke after joke with innuendos and plays on words, giving your audience no breathing space. You are a storyteller and that is what you should do. Your whole speech can be humorous from start to finish but it has to be a continuous story that you are telling – that is why a theme is so important. Even if you were to select *humour* as your theme, you would still need to describe and tell tales about the subject interspersed with jokes and anecdotes. Feel free to quote famous people, well-established epigrams or news items. When you do, the most important element is to be relevant in order to get the best response. There is a world of sayings and proverbs – even epigrams with a clever twist at the end of the short stanza – that make a statement so concise and with a wonderful insight and wit. Samuel Coleridge, the quintessential English poet, defined an epigram, asking:

> 'What is an Epigram? A dwarfish whole;
> Its body brevity, and wit its soul.'

Do not confuse an epigram with an *epigraph*, which is an inscription on a building, or with an *epitaph*, which is a text written to honour the dead. Dr Samuel Johnson is reputed to be the most quoted Englishman after Shakespeare, as recoded by his faithful friend and biographer James Boswell. I particularly enjoy his references to literature, as when he states: 'What is written without effort is in general read without pleasure.' Here is another quote close to my heart:

> 'One of the amusements of idleness is reading without the fatigue of close attention; and the world therefore swarms with writers whose wish is not to be studied, but to be read.'

His response to the advice given that books, once started, should be read all the way through, is wonderfully succinct:

> 'This is surely a strange advice; you may as well resolve that whatever men you happen to get acquainted with, you are to keep them for life. A book may be good for nothing; or there may be only one thing in it worth knowing; are we to read it all through?'

Build up a repertoire of sayings and use your favourite ones when the occasion arises. You may very well build what you have to say around the quote you like best. In any one speech, be sure not to use more than one or two quotes at the very most. To use more will detract from the relevance of the quote and reduce the impact of your statement.

Question Time

'I don't know' are the second most important three words in the world. Do not guess at an answer. Never fail to admit that you do not know the answer to a question that may be asked of you. It is not demeaning or embarrassing not to know an answer to a question. Openly admitting that you don't will gain the respect of your audience, far more so than coming up with an imprecise half-truth. The secret to knowledge is not to keep all you know in your head. The secret to knowledge is to know where to look things up. A photographic memory is very impressive and an exceedingly useful attribute, though it should not be confused with intelligence or common sense. A keen and precise memory does not necessarily mean an equally keen sense or speed of comprehension. After the lecture, do look up those subjects with which you are not familiar or to which you did not know the answer.

Audience Participation

You will be given the option to conduct a discussion, instead of giving a lecture. You need to have your audience sitting as a group and not dispersed throughout the room. Invite the brethren to sit in the East and, if necessary, arrange additional chairs around the Worshipful Master's seat so that he can remain in his place. You should also allow the secretary and treasurer to stay in their seats as they may have work to conclude. In your introduction explain that you would like your audience to participate and that you have no objections to interruptions. Your choice of subjects suitable for discussion is wide, from historical aspects of Freemasonry to current Masonic affairs. Start the discussion by asking a question relevant to the theme you are talking about. Solicit responses and then start your lecture answering or commenting on the initial responses you receive. Stop frequently and encourage additional questions. Allow yourself to deviate from your subject matter to encompass wider responses to questions asked or comments made by your audience. Keep coming back to your theme.

Theoretically, should there be no questions or comments, you should still be able to speak on your own initiative for twenty minutes to half an hour. For instance, let us take *Origins of Freemasonry* as a theoretical example for a subject matter. Here the most provocative question to start the discussion and which is bound to get a response is 'Can anyone tell me *any* theory on the origins of Freemasonry?' Someone will undoubtedly come up with the connection to Medieval Guilds and another will be the Knights Templar.

Now use both subjects raised by incorporating them into the lecture you will have prepared on the *Origins of Freemasonry*. One of the many advantages of a discussion group is that the time factor is totally flexible and you can stop at any time. Be prepared to cut the length of your lecture and keep a close eye on the time. Request the Master or Director of Ceremonies to warn you five minutes before they would like you to cease the discussion.

Ending

Always have a planned ending to your speech.

97
The recently established *World Federation of Gay Men and Women* approached the Vatican last year requesting equality in the Pope's blessings, which invariably mentioned men and women only. After considerable debate the Vatican complied with the request. On the following Sunday when the Pope stood on the balcony to address the hundreds of thousands assembled in St Peter's Square, he raised and spread his arms and intoned: 'Benedictus tutti Homini, Benedictus tutti Femini . . . Benedictus tutti Frutti.'

The story is permissible as an ending because it is amusing, inoffensive and not sexist. Even when your timing is perfect and you end exactly as planned, there may be a reason to tell one more story. Just like a concert pianist, be ready for an encore. Never tell your last story; that is, always have a group of stories in reserve. Grouping anecdotes is a good mental exercise and will serve you best when you are called upon by surprise. Have in mind stories to do with 'Daddy', 'Grandchildren', 'Lottery' or any theme you select where remembering the key word will bring to mind one or more stories on that particular theme.

Finally

Be honoured and privileged to have been asked to speak. In an interesting discussion on the subject of installed Masters' lodges with Bro Stephen Fenton – an experienced Mason and a great colleague and friend – we could not agree whether the invitation to a member to stand for election as Master of the Lodge is an honour to the brother nominated or the lodge. My own conclusion is that, more often than not, it is the new Master that feels honoured. Whereas the occasions when the lodge feels honoured are those that identify the Master Elect as a man and Mason of standing and consequence. This applies to you as speaker. The day your presence is an honour to a lodge, or any other institution that has invited you to address them, is the day that you will have reached the peak of your speaking career.

Thank you for listening to me.

98
Behind every successful man there always is . . . a surprised mother-in-law.

 99 Newspaper headlines
These are some unadulterated actual recent newspaper headlines:
Something Went Wrong in Jet Crash, Expert Says
Typhoon Rips Through Cemetery; Hundreds Dead
Miners Refuse to Work after Death
Juvenile Court to Try Shooting Defendant
War Dims Hope for Peace
If Strike Isn't Settled Quickly, It May Last A While
Cold Wave Linked to Temperatures
Enfield (London) Couple Slain; Police Suspect Homicide
Red Tape Holds Up New Bridges
Man Struck By Lightning Faces Battery Charge
New Study of Obesity Looks for Larger Test Group
Astronaut Takes Blame for Gas in Spacecraft
Kids Make Nutritious Snacks
Panda Mating Fails; Veterinarian Takes Over

100 Classics
Some classical epigrams from some classical authors:
Little strokes
Fell great oaks.
Benjamin Franklin

Here lies my wife: here let her lie!
Now she's at rest – and so am I.
John Dryden

I am His Highness' dog at Kew;
Pray tell me, sir, whose dog are you?
Alexander Pope

I'm tired of Love: I'm still more tired of Rhyme.
But Money gives me pleasure all the time.
Hilaire Belloc

I hope for nothing. I fear nothing. I am free.
Nikos Kazantzakis

101 Talking frog
It was granddad's 85th birthday. He was up at 6.30am, washed and dressed and took his customary pre-breakfast walk in the park. "Hello," he suddenly heard a high-pitched voice call out from within a bush. "It is your

birthday and I have a gift for you," the voice continued. Granddad pushed the shrub aside to find a frog that leapt straight into his outstretched hand. "If you give me a kiss," said the frog, "I will turn into a beautiful 20-year-old girl and you can do whatever you like with me." Granddad looked at the frog for a moment, and was about to slowly place it in his pocket when the frog cried out, "What are you doing?" And granddad replied, "At my age you are far more useful as a talking frog."

102 Still breathing

Three friends, men of the cloth of their respective faiths, were philosophising on the significance of death. "When I die," said the catholic priest, "and I am lying there inanimate surrounded by my friends, I would like to have them say of me 'Here was a true child of God.'" The Muslim Mufti thought for a moment and said, "When I find myself in that very same situation, I want to hear those around me say 'Here lies a true and faithful servant of Allah.'" They both looked at the rabbi, who pensively commented, "When I am lying there dead forever, surrounded by colleagues and family, I would dearly love to hear one of them cry 'My God . . . I think he is still moving.'"

103 Initiate

Bob and Bernard were inseparable from the day of their joint initiation. They went through every degree together and followed each other through the various offices in lodge, and honours were even granted to them simultaneously. Then Bob died. Bernard was inconsolable until a friend suggested that he should try a séance session. With nothing to lose Bernard agreed, and to his amazement, he made immediate contact with Bob. "How are you my old friend?" he enquired eager and excited. "I am great," replied Bob. "This is truly the Grand Lodge above in the literal sense," he explained. "We have regular meetings and festive boards and everything you could wish for. In fact, I will be attending an initiation ceremony tomorrow morning. So sorry to have to say . . . it is yours."

104 Grandma's knickers

My eight-year-old granddaughter, Issad, confidently declared that she could tell her grandmother's age. "Go on, darling," said grandma, "tell me how old I am." "I must look at your knickers," was the reply from Issad. "Why must you look at my knickers?" asked grandma. "Because *my* knickers, on the back, state 'age 6-8'."

105 Bridge on Saturdays

Rabbi Maimon is a first class bridge player and I had the occasional opportunity to partner him at duplicate competitions. Following a spiritual argument with a colleague, I enquired of him: "Rabbi, is it a sin to play bridge on the Sabbath?" He did not hesitate with his reply. "Yasha," he said. "The way you play bridge . . . is a sin at any time."

106 Chicken for dinner

Back from a hard day's work at the printing factory, I could smell the cooking as I walked through the door of my blissfully quiet home. "Hello darling, what are we having for dinner?" I enquired as I made my way to the kitchen. There was no reply. I went in and stood in the centre of the kitchen, my wife concentrating on her cooking. I asked her again, "What is it you are cooking, dear?" No response. I walked right up behind her and said loudly, "What is for dinner?" She replied, "I repeat for the third time . . . it's roast chicken."

107 Hot dogs

Arriving in America, two East European immigrants were surprised to see hot dogs for sale. Excited by the many prospects of new experiences, they decided to try it out and one of them went to the counter and returned with two hot dogs. "Look at this," he said, pointing at the open hot dog. "Out of a whole dog, this is the only bit they gave me."

108 Bar Mitzvah gift

Chaim was fast approaching his 13th birthday and asked his dad whether for this special occasion he could have a Kawasaki as a gift. Not wishing to disappoint him or show his ignorance, the father readily accepted. On the Saturday the father approached the rabbi at the synagogue and said, "I am really in a bit of a spot. My son wants a Kawasaki for his Bar Mitzvah and I am too embarrassed to tell him that I do not know what a Kawasaki is," he confessed. "I have no idea," replied the orthodox rabbi. "Why don't you ask the reform rabbi as they are a little more *au fait* with the modern world?" The father did as he was advised. "I hope you can assist me," he said to the reform rabbi. "I have agreed to make a gift of a Kawasaki for my son's Bar Mitzvah and I do not know what a Kawasaki is." The same reply came from the reform rabbi. "I have no idea either," he said. "Why don't you try the liberal rabbi? They are really with it." The father, now at the end of his tether, went up to the liberal rabbi. "I hope you can help me, rabbi," he said. "My son wants a Kawasaki for his Bar Mitzvah. Do you know what a Kawasaki is?" he asked, almost holding his breath. "Of course I do," came the reply. "A Kawasaki is a Japanese motorbike. What is a Bar Mitzvah?"

Chapter 6 summary

- Never refuse an invitation to speak
- Do not aggressively pursue opportunities
- Create the opportunity to speak
- Never apologise
- Be very cautious if you think you know it all
- Register your name as a speaker
- Always have a short speech ready
- Concentrate on one theme only
- You are not a stand-up comedian
- 'I don't know' are the most important three words
- Do not guess at an answer
- Allow audience participation
- Provoke questions and solicit responses
- Be prepared to cut the length of your lecture
- Have a planned ending
- Never tell your last story
- Feel privileged to have been asked to speak

Chapter 6 anecdotes

91 *Fat Girl Moll*
92 *Voting Waiters*
93 *Get-well Six in Favour*
94 *Privates as Deacons*
95 *Policeman Turning Green*
96 *Not as Old as I Thought*
97 *Tutti Frutti*
98 *Surprised Mum-in-Law*

Chapter 6 additional anecdotes

99   *Newspaper Headlines*
100 *Classics*
101 *Talking Frog*
102 *Still Breathing*
103 *Initiate*
104 *Grandma's Knickers*
105 *Bridge on Saturdays*
106 *Chicken for Dinner*
107 *Hot Dogs*
108 *Bar Mitzvah Gift*

CHAPTER 7

Cheeses:
Bibliography and Credits

Beresiner, Yasha *Masonic Curiosities* ANZMRC, Melbourne, 2000

Brandreth, Gyles *Cockburn's A-Z of After-dinner Entertainment*
Pelham, 1985

Carr, Harry *Masonic After-dinner proceedings: A Brief Account of Practices in the London Area* AQC 78, 1965

Cole H *Beau Brummell* Granada, London, 1977

Harris, Luke *How to Become a Powerful and Persuasive Public Speaker*
A. Thomas, London, 1972

Jackson, A. C. F. *Our Predecessors of About the Time that Quatuor Coronati Lodge was Founded* AQC 90

Minkoff, David *The Ultimate Book of Jewish Jokes* Robson, London, 2005

Monkhouse, Bob *Just Say a Few Words* Lennard, London, 1988

Pronchnow , Herbert *The Public Speakers Treasure Chest*
A. Thomas, London, 1977

Smyth, Frederick *A Reference Book for Freemasons* QCCC London, 1998

I am indebted to friends and family for support and assistance:

John Hart, congratulating him on his 50th year as a Freemason and acknowledging his first-hand experience and guidance.

Graeme Living, a soul mate, loyal and good friend, much lamented.

Sheila Pusinelli, who deserved acknowledgement long before now for the many occasions that she read my manuscripts and for going through this script in such meticulous detail.

Graham Redman, for his ready advice and unsurpassed knowledge of our Masonic Constitutions.

Ralph Wheeler, very long standing excellent friend, Masonic organiser and lecturer.

Dana Wolf, my darling daughter for feeding me dozens of super stories, especially true ones about Dassi, Tali, Michaeli and Shirale.

Leo Zanelli, exceptional friend and colleague, for putting me right, of all things, on protocol.

Overeating can cause nightmares
Humphrey *c*1800 (Guildhall)

About the author:

Yasha Beresiner was born in Turkey in 1940, had his primary education in England and is a Faculty of Law graduate of the Hebrew University of Jerusalem. He settled in London in 1969. He is a City of London Guide and the editor of the *City Guides' and Lecturers' Association* magazine. He has been an active Freemason since 1975 and holds Grand Rank in England, Italy and Israel. He is a Past Master of the Quatuor Coronati lodge, the Premier lodge of Masonic Research. In 1980 he converted his hobbies to a full-time business and is currently writing, consulting and trading in collectables through his website www.intercol.co.uk.

By the same author:

The Paper Tiger Stayman, 1968 (Arab-Israeli 1967 War)
Catalogue of Colombian Currency Stanley Gibbons, 1972
The Story of Paper Money David & Charles, 1976
Collectors' Guide to Paper Money Andre Deutsch/Stein, 1979
British County Maps – A Guide ACC Woodbridge, 1985
Masonic Curiosities and more... ANZMRC Victoria, Australia, 2000
Royal Arch: 4th Degree of the Antients Batham lecture 2000
   (sponsored by the Supreme Grand Chapter Of England)
City of London – A Masonic Guide Lewis Masonic, 2006

CHAPTER 8

Petits Fours:
Appendices

Appendix 1

Modes of Address, Honours and Decorations

Her Majesty The Queen – Your Majesty, Ma'am
His Royal Highness The Duke of Edinburgh – Your Royal Highness, Sir
His Royal Highness, The Prince of Wales – Your Royal Highness, Sir
Her Royal Highness, The Princess Royal – Your Royal Highness, Ma'am
Sarah, Duchess of York – Madam
Duke/Duchess – Duke/Duchess
Eldest son of a Duke – Lord
Marquess/Marchioness – Lord/Lady
Earl/Countess – Lord/Lady
Viscount/Viscountess – Lord/Lady
Life Peer – Lord
Knight – Sir
Wife of a Knight – Lady
The Lord Chancellor – Right Honourable
Lords of Appeal – Right Honourable
Judges of the High Court – The Honourable
Lords Justices of Appeal – Lord or Lady Justice
Judges of the High Court – Mr or Mrs Justice
The Pope – His Holiness
Cardinals – His Eminence
Bishops – Your Excellency
Priest – Father
Rabbi – Rabbi
Foreign Ambassador – Excellency
United Nations Ambassador – Mister
Generals, Lt Generals and Major-Generals – General
Colonels and Lt Colonels – Colonel
Staff Sergeants and Colour Sergeants – Staff or Colour

Abbreviations of Honours in order of precedence.

The list is not comprehensive.

Bt/Bart	Baronet
VC	Victoria Cross
GC	George Cross
KG/LG	Knight/Lady of the Most Noble Order of the Garter
KT/LT	Knight/Lady of the Most Ancient and Most Noble Order of the Thistle
PC	Privy Counsellor
GCB	(Knight/Dame) Grand Cross of the Most Honourable Order of the Bath
OM	Member of the Order of Merit
GCMG	Knight/Dame Grand Cross of the Most Distinguished Order of Saint Michael and Saint George
GCVO	Knight/Dame Grand Cross of the Royal Victorian Order
GBE	Knight/Dame Grand Cross of the Most Excellent Order of the British Empire
CH	Member of the Order of the Companions of Honour
KCMG	Knight/Dame Commander of the Most Distinguished Order of Saint Michael and Saint George
KCVO	Knight or Dame Commander of the Royal Victorian Order
KBE/DBE	Knight or Dame Commander of the Most Excellent Order of the British Empire
CB	Companion of the Most Honourable Order of the Bath
CMG	Companion of the Most Distinguished Order of Saint Michael and Saint George
CVO	Commander of the Royal Victorian Order
CBE	Commander of the Most Excellent Order of the British Empire
DSO	Companion of the Distinguished Service Order
OBE	Officer of the Most Excellent Order of the British Empire
ISO	Companion of the Imperial Service Order
MBE	Member of the Most Excellent Order of the British Empire
MC	Military Cross
DCM	Distinguished Conduct Medal
GM	George Medal
DSM	Distinguished Service Medal
QGM	Queen's Gallantry Medal
BEM	British Empire Medal

Appendix 2
Masonic Ranks

When addressing Masonic dignitaries present, those of the rank of 'Most Worshipful', 'Right Worshipful' and/or 'Very Worshipful' should be singled out after the 'Worshipful Master'. Clause 6 of our *Book of Constitutions* gives the details as well as the appropriate salutations:

Titles, prefixes and abbreviations
The prefixes to be accorded to and used by brethren are as follows:

Most Worshipful (MW):
The Grand Master, Pro Grand Master, Past Grand Masters and Past Pro Grand Masters.

Right Worshipful (RW):
Present and Past Deputy Grand Masters, Assistant Grand Masters, Provincial and District Grand Masters, Pro Provincial, District Grand Masters and Grand Wardens.

Very Worshipful (VW):
Present and Past Grand Chaplains, Presidents of the Board of General Purposes, Grand Registrars, Grand Secretaries, Presidents of the Board of Benevolence, Presidents of the Grand Charity, Presidents of the Masonic Foundation for the Aged and the Sick, Presidents of the Masonic Trust for Girls and Boys, Grand Directors of Ceremonies, Grand Sword Bearers, Grand Superintendents of Works, and Grand Inspectors.

Provided always those members of the Grand Lodge who at the date of this amendment coming to operation (20 April 1969) held the offices of Grand Treasurer, Past Grand Treasurer, Deputy Grand Registrar or Past Deputy Grand Registrar shall continue to be described as 'Very Worshipful'.

Worshipful (W):
Other Grand Officers, present and past, and Masters of lodges, present and past. All other brethren shall have the style of 'brother' only.

The Salutes when given shall be as follows:
MW brethren – eleven; the Deputy and Assistant Grand Masters, present and past – nine; other RW brethren – seven; VW brethren – five; other Grand Officers, present and past – three.

Within their own Provinces and Districts (and the Metropolitan Grand Lodge of London), present Deputy and Assistant Provincial, District (and Metropolitan) Grand Masters – five, and other Provincial, District (and Metropolitan) Grand Officers, present and past – three. In London holders of Senior London and London Grand Rank – three; and in lodges abroad not under Districts, holders of Overseas Grand Rank – three.

Appendix 3

Toast List

The Recommended Toast List is as follows. Note that in London and in each of the Provinces, the correct and appropriate names will be inserted as needed.

1. The Queen and The Craft

2. The Most Worshipful The Grand Master:
HIS ROYAL HIGHNESS THE DUKE OF KENT

3. The Most Worshipful Pro Grand Master:
THE MOST HONOURABLE THE MARQUESS OF NORTHAMPTON

The Right Worshipful Deputy Grand Master:
PETER GEOFFREY LOWNDES

The Right Worshipful Assistant Grand Master:
DAVID KENNETH WILLIAMSON
and the rest of the Grand Officers, Present and Past

4. The Right Worshipful Metropolitan or Provincial Grand Master:
NAMED IN FULL

5. The Deputy Metropolitan or Provincial Grand Master:
NAMED IN FULL

The Assistant Metropolitan or Provincial Grand Masters:
LISTED AND NAMED IN FULL
and the rest of the Officers of Metropolitan or Provincial Grand Lodge,
Present and Past

6. The Worshipful Master

7. Absent brethren

8. The Visiting brethren

9. The Tyler's Toast

CHAPTER 9

Natural Sparkling Spring Water:
Post Script

An improbable (though essentially true) autobiography of the author:

109
On 12 June 1940, I was born in Istanbul, Turkey, in such a state of shock that I did not speak for the next two years.

As if that was not enough, being born to a Jewish family, the ceremony of my circumcision took place just a week later.

110
It has oft been stated that this is the sign of an optimistic race, happy to cut a piece off before knowing how long it will be.

111
Many years later my army colleague and close friend Danny decided to convert to Judaism, preoccupied only by the prospect of the circumcision he had to undergo to complete his conversion. "Is it painful?" he asked me, with tense concern visible in his features. "Painful?" I repeated.
"I was circumcised when I was just eight days old . . . and did not walk for 18 months."

In 1948 my dad, following a tramway accident, was hospitalised in Italy and I was deposited in an Israeli kibbutz, Ben Shemen, for 12 months. When I joined my parents and younger brother in Milan, I was just nine years old, and the only school my parents could initially place me in was La Scuola Cattolica del Sacro Cuore. I was warmly welcomed as the only Jewish boy, one of the chosen, in the Catholic school. It was here that I learned the quaint rhyme:

> *How odd of God*
> *To choose the Jews*
> *Not half as odd, by God*
> *As the gentiles*
> *A Jewish God to choose.*

I have memories of some wonderful moments and several awful half-hours. One tearful memory remains imbedded in my mind.

✡ 112

Miss Camellia, our gentle religious studies teacher, was preparing to send us kids home at the end of the scholastic day: "What were you doing, Paolo?" she asked of my eight-year-old colleague. "I was playing with the ball with Maria in the garden," he replied. The teacher said, "Well, if you can spell the word 'ball' correctly, you can go home early this afternoon." And Paolo spelled 'ball' to perfection. Next up was Maria, as she came in through the garden doors. Miss Camellia asked her exactly the same question and she replied, "I was in the sand playing with Paolo." Once again, the teacher replied, "If you can spell the word 'sand', you can go home early." Maria had no difficulties with her spelling. My turn was next, and with tears pouring down my cheeks, I cried, "I was also out there with Maria and Paolo but they would not play with me because I am Jewish." "What?" exclaimed Miss Camellia with considerable alarm. "That is prejudicial discrimination. If you can spell 'prejudicial discrimination' you, too, can go home early today, Yasha."

Without a doubt, the greatest influence on my life has been my father. He was a wonderful, warm man and highly successful in business.

✡ 113

I could not have been more than seven or eight when I declared that when I grew up I wanted to become a prophet. "No, my son," my father corrected me. "When you grow up, you want to make a profit."

I was grasping the concept.

✡ 114

At maths class the teacher once asked me, "How much is 5%?" To which I replied, "I agree entirely teacher, how much is 5%?"

In 1953, I was sent to prep school in Northwood, Middlesex, run by Lawrence Beesley: one of the Titanic's last survivors. He succeeded in getting me into Embley Park, the public school in Romsey, Hampshire, where the wild gardens were grounds shared with Lord Mountbatten's estate. I only saw my parents on the occasional holiday and enjoyed my dad's wisdom and explanations to the ways of the world.

✡ 115

"Why did God invent gentiles?" I asked on one occasion. His reply, as always, was immediate and logical: "Someone's got to buy retail," he responded.

✡ 116

"What is honesty, Dad?" I ventured. To which his response was by way of an example: "Suppose you make a £50 sale in your shop. You wrap the item and the customer leaves happy and satisfied. However, you discover that he has mistakenly handed you two £50 notes. This is where the question of honesty comes up," he explained. "Do you tell your partner or don't you?"

During his whole commercial career, my dad only had one partner who was quaintly named Fiefield.

117

Fiefield liked everything in cash, and so, a large safe was rented from a bank where the money could be deposited. A couple of weeks later, Fiefield said to my dad: "I think we should check the money in the safe," and off he went to the bank. Within minutes my dad received a phone call. "You will not believe this!" an agitated Fiefield was shouting down the line. "All the money has gone! The safe is empty! I have called the police! Inform the insurance company!" "Fiefield," my father replied in a calm voice. "Fiefield. Calm down and put the money back, please."

From a young age I chose law as my profession, notwithstanding my dad's ambition that I should join his business. At one stage of his commercial career, he had an extraordinary shop selling electrical equipment, as well as stamps and paintings, among other things. On my holidays I used to sit and watch in awe as he conducted his business.

118

I remember the day when he sold no fewer than five large paintings to various customers. "How much is that oil painting?" asked the first customer, who began a long session of bargaining. "This is my last offer," said my father. "That painting cost me £150 and you can have it at cost." The second and third customers enjoyed a similar privilege. The paintings cost £200 and £250 respectively and he sold them at cost. At the end of the day I asked the logical question. "Dad, how can you survive if you sell your paintings at cost?" I queried. "Today, my son, I taught you how to sell at cost," he explained. "Tomorrow, I will teach you how to buy below cost."

In 1958 I returned to Israel and volunteered into the famed 890 Parachute Regiment spending two exciting, if somewhat apprehensive years in the forces. The only benefit greater than maturing from boy to man was my meeting with the sergeant major in the Hebrew School at the Schneller base in Jerusalem. In 1963 she became my wife, Arimz.

119

The only other such instance I am aware of is with the Grenadier Guards, the British Military Regiment, in which the Colonel is married to the Colonel-in-Chief: The Duke of Edinburgh and Queen Elizabeth II respectively.

Pass The Port
USA Are You a Mason? postcard series 1920s

I was a married student teaching judo and English whilst enrolled in the Hebrew University of Jerusalem, where I finally received my LLB (Bachelor of Law degree) in 1968, and in 1969, we moved to England.

We have never been a religious family – as is the case with a majority of Israelis, we celebrate many of our biblical traditions in a secular environment. We light candles on Fridays without fully-fledged prayers; we fast on the Day of Atonement (Yom Kippur) without spending time in the synagogue; we celebrate a week-long Chanukah festival and give gifts when we need not. We do so because our festival of lights invariably precedes Christmas by a week or so, and it is only fair on our children, whose Christian friends enjoy Christmas gifts, that they too should be so blessed. In a wonderful display of love and unity between religions and race, the community in Golders Green annually enjoys 'Chanumas'. A fully lit Christmas tree stands by the large seven branch Chanukah candelabra, each branch alight with the flickering flame of another festive day. Priests and rabbis bless the children and tell tales appropriate to each community's long-standing traditions.

120
A rabbi and his Catholic priest best friend finally reached that stage of intimacy in their relationship that allowed the priest to ask: "Truthfully now Rabbi, have you ever eaten pork?" "Yes, I will admit it," replied the rabbi. "I did

so once, but it was totally inadvertently and I have no doubt that I have been forgiven. Now be honest with me, have you ever been with a woman?" the rabbi asked. "God forbid!" cried the Catholic priest. "You should try it out," said the rabbi. "It is much better than eating pork."

Notwithstanding our rare attendance at the local synagogue, in which we are paid-up members, we have become friendly with our Rabbi Maimon Zeltner for many decades. Each synagogue guards the interests of its membership as if it were a secret organisation of consequence.

121

When I wanted to speak to my dad on a Saturday morning and knew that he was attending his own Edgware Road synagogue, I was surprised not to be allowed in by the Shamash – equivalent to a Tyler or outside guard – because I was not a member of that particular synagogue. "I only want to have a few words with my dad," I insisted. "He is expecting me and I have a message for him. I only want to talk to him." This was all to no avail until the rabbi came out of his room. I explained that I was not a member, would only greet my father, and leave in a few moments. The rabbi finally consented. "Just five minutes," he said. "And I better not catch you praying whilst you are in there."

122

Many years ago, I met Rabbi Maimon in his office at the Temple Fortune Synagogue to discuss my son Yug's Bar Mitzvah. As we started our conversation, a phone call came through and I witnessed the following exchange:

"Is that Rabbi Maimon speaking?" I heard a stern voice at the other end of the line ask.
"It is," came the reply.
"This is the Inland Revenue. Do you have a Mr and Mrs Goldman in your congregation?"
"We have."
"Have they been fully paid-up members of the synagogue since 1995?"
"They have."
"Did the Goldmans contribute £53,768.22 to the synagogue welfare fund in the last year?"
"They will . . ." replied Rabbi Maimon, after only a moment's hesitation.

A Bar Mitzvah is a grand occasion for a Jewish family that begins in the synagogue in the morning, continues all day and ends with a bustling home party in the evening.

123

I had contacted the caterers and said that I wanted something different, original and outstanding for my son's Bar Mitzvah and no expense was to be spared. That evening at the reception, in the middle of the room on an elevated platform, stood a truly magnificent and detailed half-bust sculpture of Yug . . . made entirely of chopped liver. As the evening wore on and our guests tucked into the liver, the figure eventually disintegrated and collapsed. It was with some shock that a couple of days later I received an invoice from the caterers that read: 'Bar Mitzvah boy chopped liver sculpture: £5,250'. "Is this a joke or an error?" I complained on the phone to the manager of the catering company. "Sir, we had to employ a qualified artist to sculpt your boy's head and shoulders," the manager explained. "What are you talking about? This was chopped liver," I said exasperated. "For £5,000 I could get Henry Moore to do my son's head." "I am very sorry, sir," he replied. "Henry Moore only works with egg and onions."

Rabbi Maimon officiated at Yug's Bar Mitzvah and many other events in my family. It was natural for me to send my daughter Anad to seek his advice when, to our great surprise, she decided to marry Edualc, a charming Jewish orthodox boy. It was the fact that he was orthodox that surprised us. I still insist that he cannot be that orthodox having married my very secular daughter, brought up in a very secular Jewish environment. Nevertheless they decided to marry.

124

Anad's concerns when she met with Rabbi Maimon were various and quite natural. "Are we permitted to make love before the wedding?" she asked Rabbi Maimon innocently. The rabbi's response was typical of his approach to life and Judaism: "As long as you are not late for the ceremony, there is no problem."

125

In a similar vein, Anad wanted to know the restrictions that orthodox Judaism would impose on her. "Nothing is different to what you have been used to, even in a secular Jewish environment," Rabbi Maimon assured her. "All you will have to get used to is a stricter application of biblical rules and regulations with which you are already familiar." "For instance?" asked my daughter. "For instance," the rabbi continued, "on your wedding night you will not be allowed to dance with your own husband. Men dance with men and women with women, apart from one another." "Does that mean," asked my rather disconcerted daughter, "that when we make love, I always have to lie on my back?" Only slightly embarrassed by the question, the rabbi responded, "No my child, there is nothing in the Sacred Book that forbids you from variety in your intimacy." Somewhat relieved, Anad persisted, "You mean we could do it standing up, somewhere?" "No!" the rabbi said, now alarmed. "Standing up is out of the question. It could lead to dancing."

126

My natural concern when I met Edualc for the first time, was with finances. "Edualc, you want to marry this summer and you still don't have a

job," I pointed out. "What are your plans?" "I am totally confident in my trust
in the Almighty," Edualc replied, symbolically placing his hand on his scull cap.
"That is fine," I insisted, "but you will need finances to purchase a house.
It will not take long before you have children, you will need money." "Please do
not worry," Edualc said with total confidence. "God will guide me. God will
help me. God will provide. I know it." I had no choice but to concede. I shook
him warmly by the hand and wished him good luck and a long life. When
Arimz asked me what I thought of our son-in-law to be, I had to be honest.
"I like him," I replied. "I have only known him 15 minutes and he is already
calling me God."

In 1975, when I was initiated into Freemasonry, my life changed in many
ways – I genuinely felt that as a good man I could become a better one. That
sentiment satisfied a spiritual need in me. In addition, the history of the
ancient Craft dating back some 300 years very much appealed to my sense of
curiosity as a budding historian. The universal, international appeal of the
Society was also of great interest. At the time, I was travelling on business all
over the world, and my six languages allowed me to attend lodges in countries ranging from Nigeria to Monaco. The familiarity of the Masonic ritual
allowed me to understand what was being said even when I could not speak
the language. Israel and Italy came particularly close to my heart and I have
been privileged to have been awarded high honours from both jurisdictions.

In 1993, at the mature age of 78, my dad decided to become a Freemason
to enable him to join me on my lectures and tours. He took to Freemasonry
like a duck takes to water. He enjoyed every minute in the lodge room and
we became closer friends through him joining the Craft.

127
At 80 he once said: "I have now reached that age when everything hurts
and whatever does not hurt does not work," he added. "Whenever I bend down, I
think to myself . . . is there anything else I can do whilst I am down here."

His great pride was his excellent eyesight. On my visit to his home in
Marbella, Spain, in April 1995, we went round the golf course as we had
done at infrequent intervals.

128
On this occasion, I commented that whilst my drive off the tee had
improved a great deal, my failing eyesight was becoming a major handicap as
I kept losing golf balls. "Don't worry, Yasha," said my dad. "Hit the ball as well
as you can and I will keep an eye on it. I may be 80," he added with pride,
"but I still have 20/20 vision." I had the best drive off the tee ever: a wonderful
co-ordinated swing – the perfect golf shot. The ball must have flown 320
yards towards the green. "Did you see where that went, Dad?" I asked eager
to hear that my drive was as majestic as it had felt. "Of course I did," he replied
without further comment. "Well?" I prompted eagerly. "Where did the ball go?"
After a moment's hesitation, my dad replied, "I don't remember!"

Our most memorable Masonic trips were to Israel. We flew El Al (Every Landing Always Late) whenever we could.

129
On the last occasion we travelled there together, a year before he passed to the Grand Lodge above in 1995, we were guests at the birthday party of the mother of the Unknown Soldier.

130
The next day, together with dignitaries from all over Israel, we attended the unveiling ceremony of the statue to the Unknown Soldier. It was an impressive gathering: the Mayor of Tel Aviv, the Army's Chief of Staff, our own Grand Master, soldiers, Masonic dignitaries and a gathering of curious and interested citizens. As the veil was lifted from the impressive sculpture of a soldier, his Uzi machine gun in hand in a defiant and victorious stance, I noted the sculpted text above his head. It read 'Dov Zeltnik – Unknown Soldier'. I turned to the official-looking gentleman standing next to me and said, "This does not make sense. How can he be the 'unknown soldier' if he is named Dov Zeltnik?" "It is perfectly logical," said my companion. "Dov Zeltnik was a very famous tailor, but as a soldier," he explained, "he was completely unknown."

I understood the concept, having selected logical studies as one of my subjects at university.

131
I remember trying to explain to my friend Conrad what logic studies entailed. I thought the best way to do it was, as my father had taught me, by way of example. "Do you have a fish tank in your home?" I asked Conrad. "Yes," he replied. "Well, if you have a fish tank, it is perfectly logical to conclude that you also have fish in your home," I explained. "But logic extends way beyond that simple statement," I continued. "If you have fish it would be logical to presume that you also have other pets." I noted Conrad's nod of approval. "And if you have pets you are likely to have children, if you have children you must have a wife, and the final logical conclusion to that is that if you have a wife you cannot be a homosexual," I stated almost triumphantly. A week later I overheard Conrad explaining to his colleague the essence of logic. "Do you have a fish tank?" asked Conrad in anticipation. "No," replied his colleague. "In that case you must be a homosexual," Conrad concluded.

132
On our return flight to London, a group of ultra orthodox Jews were justifying the content of their suitcase to a customs officer. "Why do you have so many sets of false teeth?" asked the officer. "Well you see, it is like this, sir," explained the senior member of the group. "In our religion we are not allowed to mix meat and milk products. So I use the blue silver false teeth when eating

milky products and I use the gold red set when eating meat." "What about the platinum set?" the officer asked. "That one, officer," the Hassid replied, "is for when I sometimes have an irresistible urge to eat a ham sandwich."

It is a curious fact that today, in this very liberated society, homosexuality is little known in Israel.

133
Famously, a Jewish boy persuades his friend to lie next to him and gently whispers in his ear, "Turn over." After a moment's thought, his friend replies, "About 400,000 a year."

According to Masonic legend as well as biblical lore, the Holy Land is the cradle of civilisation and Freemasonry. Modern Freemasonry began with the formation of the Grand Lodge of the State of Israel in 1953 following on a century of Masonic activity in the area under various jurisdictions including Italian, Egyptian and Palestinian. Today some 2000 brethren of all faiths meet in 80 lodges spread from Rosh Hanikra on the northern border with Lebanon, to Eilat in the southern tip of the country. We enjoy regular Freemasonry in eight languages. Israel is recognised by all major Masonic jurisdictions worldwide. Our ladies, more often than not, join our festive boards following the lodge meeting. Business is conducted Scottish style, because Israel was sponsored and consecrated by the Grand Lodge of Scotland and our festive boards have the usual toasts and speeches. The stories and tales have as much Jewish flavour as they have other ethnic ones.

134
The Sultan of Brunei, the richest man in the world, was seeking assistance from anyone who may have had his own exceedingly rare TC(a-) blood type. Hundreds of letters and e-mails were sent out, announcements made and even the media alerted but to no avail. Until, that is, Giora Shabtai of Petach Tiqva was informed and was happy to donate, without hesitation or consideration, two pints of blood. Two weeks later, Giora received a telephone call from his excited and incredulous bank manager: "Mr Shabtai, I do not know how you did it but we have just credited your account with one million US dollars. Congratulations!" Giora explained the circumstances and spent the next twelve months living like a king. He met the sultan on a few occasions, took holidays in the Caribbean and bought himself a home in Caesarea, the posh district in Israel. Predictably, Giora ran out of money. Two months later an e-mail from the sultan asked if Giora was in a position to be able to assist again. Without hesitation, Giora had five pints of his blood delivered to the Sultan the next day at his own expense. He now waited. When a couple of months had gone by, he telephoned his bank to check whether any funds had been credited to his account. "Nothing special, Mr Shabtai," said the bank manager. "US$500 from Brunei. I did not think I needed to bother you about

it." Giora was as disappointed as he was mystified. In his wisdom he decided to call the sultan. They had, after all, met on a couple of occasions. "Sultan," Giora said in a pensive tone of voice, "I want to tell you that this has nothing to do with money. It is my curiosity that I need to satisfy. Before, I sent you two pints of blood and you sent me $1,000,000. Now I sent you five pints and you send me $500. I really would like to understand." "My friend, the explanation is simple," replied the Sultan. "Before, I did not have any Jewish blood in me."

Lazi, my father, became a close friend when we began to share our experiences as Freemasons. On 8 April 1995, I received a phone call from him in Spain, saying that he wanted to come to London for no particular reason. The Passover festivities were approaching and we were delighted to have him home. We went to play bridge at the Acol Club in West End Lane, Hampstead, and during a game, Lazi – who had suffered from lifelong diabetes – complained that he was feeling ill. On the way home, he asked if I should take him to Barnet Hospital. Rather than risk his confinement to a hospital over the holiday period, I called a doctor who arrived at my home at 3.00am. The doctor confirmed that Lazi's sugar levels were low and prescribed a jam sandwich for him to eat and then go to bed.

The next morning, Lazi got up early, shaved, dressed smart as was his habit, and on the landing between my study and our bedroom one floor below, he sat on the top step, placed his head against the wall and went to sleep forever. We saw him when we came out of our bedroom, probably within half an hour of his passing. He had a serene half-smile on his face. That was Friday 9 April. The next day his ticket won £10 in the National Lottery. I have always felt that coincidence was a special send-off, like a pretty bow tie engulfing a whole lifetime. I will forever visualise him sitting in heaven on that fateful Saturday, flanked by Elvis Presley (why not?), looking down on us and thinking to himself 'Thank goodness I did not win £100,000!'

It was only two short years after his initiation that he passed to the Grand Lodge above. I earnestly believe that he died a happier man for having become a Freemason . . . just as I will. Will you too?

CHAPTER 10

Wines & Liqueurs:
Indices

Reference is made in these indexes to the anecdote numbers, not page numbers

Index A: *Anecdotes in alphabetical order*

Index B: *Anecdotes by subject matter*